# ASTRAL
## PROJECTION
### PLAIN & SIMPLE

*. . . spiritual teaching which is right for you will generally hold one drop of wholesome bitters in the sweetness. It will call you to rise a little higher than you wanted to go just yet. That may be the very reason you needed to hear it . . .*

—Osborne Phillips

## About the Author

Osborne Phillips is a long-time student of the occult, involved with paranormal disciplines for thirty-six years. He is coauthor, with the late Melita Denning, of a number of books in Llewellyn's Practical Guide series, the Magical Philosophy series, and other titles.

Phillips is a recognized authority on the Western Mystery Tradition, teaching and making the study of magick accessible through his writing. He studied under such teachers as U Maung Maung Ji, an associate of Mahatma Gandhi. He is also a student of Jungian psychology. Phillips has worked in the western esoteric Order Aurum Solis since the age of sixteen. He lived for a time in the United States, but currently makes his home in his native England.

## To Write to the Author

If you wish to contact the author or would like more information about this book, please write to the author in care of Llewellyn Worldwide and we will forward your request. Both the author and publisher appreciate hearing from you and learning of your enjoyment of this book and how it has helped you. Llewellyn Worldwide cannot guarantee that every letter written to the author can be answered, but all will be forwarded. Write to:

Osborne Phillips
C/o Llewellyn Worldwide
P.O. Box 64383, Dept. 0-7387-0279-X
St. Paul, MN 55164-0383, U.S.A.

Please enclose a self-addressed stamped envelope for reply, or $1.00 to cover costs.
If outside U.S.A., enclose international postal reply coupon.

Many of Llewellyn's authors have websites with additional information and resources. For more information, please visit our website at:
http://www.llewellyn.com

# ASTRAL
# PROJECTION
# PLAIN & SIMPLE

## THE OUT-OF-BODY EXPERIENCE

## OSBORNE PHILLIPS

2003
Llewellyn Publications
St. Paul, Minnesota 55164-0383, U.S.A.

FIRST EDITION
Second Printing, 2003

Book interior design and editing by Connie Hill
Cover design by Kevin R. Brown
Cover image © 2002 by Photodisc

Library of Congress Cataloging-in-Publication Data

Phillips, Osborne.
    Astral projection plain & simple : the out-of-body experience / Osborne Phillips.
    — 1st ed.
        p.   cm.
    Includes index.
    ISBN 0-7387-0279-X
    1. Astral projection.   I. Title: Astral projection plain and simple.   II. Title.

BF1389.A7 P49    2003
133.9'5—dc21                                                        2002040562

Llewellyn Publications
A Division of Llewellyn Worldwide, Ltd.
P.O. Box 64383, Dept. 0-7387-0279-X
St. Paul, MN  55164-0383, U.S.A.
www.llewellyn.com

Printed in the United States of America

# Books by Osborne Phillips

# Contents

# Astral Techniques

# Foreword

Whoever you are, wherever you are, there's a great life waiting for you—a lot of great lives—and you don't have to die to get them. That's part of the wonder and splendor of it, and it's waiting there for you now, at this present time.

## Come out and play!

Perhaps most of your days you sit at a desk, your moments of daydreaming spent in counting the months and the dollars to the glowing annual burst of vacation freedom.

Perhaps you are a homemaker, putting up a secret struggle to keep those wide horizons of imagination open for yourself and your partner until the kids are grown.

Or your job may involve lots of travel, and you may just long for the time to explore some of the places of which you catch such tantalizing glimpses. Or you may be an astronomer for whom the far sight of the cosmic glories is no longer enough. Or you may be a prisoner to a hospital bed or to a wheelchair. Or you may, for that matter, be in jail. Or you may be simply a dreamer, wishing your dreams could be something more than only dreams, with all their fantastic happenings.

*Whoever you are, come on out!*

## Another kind of freedom?

It may be another kind of freedom that you long for. You may have read books on religion, on philosophy, psychology, the occult—any or all of these subjects—and you may have wished very deeply that you could see beyond the conflicting viewpoints, to have your own experience of the unseen worlds, to be able to draw your own conclusions on these matters.

Is there life after death?—you may have asked yourself.

What about reincarnation?

Who am "I"? Who have I been? What can I become?

What can I do to help myself? To help others?

Can I do these things while making the most of my present life?

You can discover the answers to these questions and comprehend them in terms of your own living experience.

## This book: what is its "line?"

This book does not set out to teach any particular system of religion or of philosophy, although if you have knowledge of a particular system you may, through this book, gain insight into some of its underlying truths. This book sets out to take you into the great psychic art of astral projection, an art that is a natural part of your birthright as a human being.

It is as natural as the will to live. As natural as dreaming. As natural as the impulse to self-expression in image-making, dancing, music, acting, every creative art.

It is as natural as the certainty that we ought somehow to be able to fly without aircraft: the certainty that brings to dreams of free-flying such a deep feeling of happiness and fulfillment.

## Your potential

Discover how much astral projection offers you. It will show you the reality of much that had seemed beyond human vision and knowledge.

It will open up for you the mysteries of the past and the future. It will whirl you to unsuspected heights of sexual ecstasy and fulfillment. It will empower you to explore the wonders of the world, to look into the marvelous potential of your psyche, to help others overcome the seeming limitations that beset them; and it will give you access to the shining vistas beyond—the infinite levels and dimensions of the astral world.

# 1

# What Is Astral?

The astral world or plane covers a wide range of reality. In its highest reaches it gives form to what is spiritual and helps make a thought thinkable. At its lower levels it is so close to the physical universe that a dividing line cannot easily be maintained. It includes our astral bodies, the soul-stuff of the individual psyche.

## Etheric sight in ordinary consciousness

The lower levels of the astral world are sometimes termed "etheric." Many people, without leaving their physical body at all, can make use of "etheric sight"—the power to see the colors, forms, and living beings of at least the lower astral levels. With practice, you can almost certainly cultivate this power of seeing. It is a knack. It has nothing whatever to do with the sharpness or other aspects of your physical eyesight. It has nothing to do with virtue, either. Sometimes people who declare they can see nonmaterial beings are treated as if they were claiming to be holy, or somehow spiritually gifted. In fact the only virtues needed for etheric sight are attentiveness and open-mindedness.

Certainly the level of one's awareness of the astral is governed by one's state of inner readiness; but that too can be developed, and aspiration generally grows in proportion to the knowledge of something to aspire to.

## The senses in astral consciousness

When you are out of your body you will, of course, see, hear, and be generally aware of what is around you. Every manifestation of being is real and palpable at its own level. If you travel astrally at the level of the material world you will see it as it is at that time—if that is what you wish—although you are likely to perceive more of its past, and perhaps of its future, than earthly traveling would show you. As an astral being you will be able to pass directly through a solid earthly wall or closed door with no trouble, no matter how solid or closed it may look.

At some time when you are out of the body, however, you may well encounter some high astral boundary that is not for you to pass as yet—for it, being astral, too, and of a higher astral potency, is solid and effective at astral level.

## Body and psyche

Not to get too technical: "you," an intelligent consciousness, are the unifying focal point in a combination of body and psyche. Body and psyche alike follow your conscious will to a great extent, but both have their deep reticences—areas in which they pursue their own life outside your knowledge or control.

When you, the intelligent consciousness, fare forth to out-of-the-body experience, how much of the psyche is thus temporarily separated from the main organism? It feels to you just like your physical body. Is it, then, your entire astral body, the totality of your animating soul-stuff?

No, it is not! You can depend upon your breathing and heart-action to continue steadily while you are out; and you, the roving consciousness, however remote and adventurous your travels, never lose your way back. Like the hero of a thriller, you always get home safe again. All these safeguards are functions of the stay-at-home part of your astral body.

## Traveling light

At the same time, your consciousness does not go out alone and naked into the astral world. It needs—*you* need—a certain amount of astral substance to gather impressions and information for it. Astral substance performs this function very well, as it habitually mediates between the physical nervous systems and the psyche.

Inevitably, too, this astral substance that fares forth with your consciousness, since it comes from the instinctual and emotional region of your psyche, will carry some of your customary feelings and reactions; all of which helps to make you feel complete and thoroughly yourself in your travels.

Fortunately, any person in a tolerable state of health has more than enough astral substance to spare, without robbing what is needed to keep the body's necessary services running meanwhile. Your astral body is, in any case, continually giving off small quantities of its substance and replenishing from outer sources; a person in vigorous psychic health, even without great bodily strength, gives off so much astral substance that even bystanders may perceive it: "electrical vitality," or "vibrant personality," they comment.

The probability is that when you first begin to project your consciousness from your physical body, you'll take considerably more astral substance with you than you need.

With more practice you'll begin to travel light.

The soul-stuff is remarkably elastic and expansive, and a small portion of it is enough to give an experienced astral traveler the feeling, and far more than the faculties, of the earthly body.

## Astral substance: one kind only

The part of the astral body most closely engaged with the physical body is described as the "gross astral," on account of its greater density. Gross astral substance as such is not usually taken for purposes of projection: it may be taken by accident, as by a beginner, or for a specific purpose, as a physical medium can do to ensure its visibility to a minimally clairvoyant audience.

This does not mean however that gross astral substance is essentially different from the general kind. Air at sea level is not essentially different from air on a mountain peak. The air at sea level is denser, but if the wind carries it to the high peaks it becomes at once as rarefied as any other air at that altitude. Astral substance is far more elastic and more swiftly circulating than air. To say therefore that gross astral substance is not usually taken out by the experienced traveler is not a statement as to the *part* of the astral body from which it is taken—the astral body does not really have parts—but simply refers to the condition of the substance when taken out.

## The same all over!

The fact that there is only one kind of astral substance has some interesting and exciting consequences.

Each and every organ of your physical body—eyes, nose, ears, and so on—has its counterpart in the astral body. This does not mean that the different areas of your astral body are limited in function like the corresponding parts of your physical body. The whole of your astral body, or any particle of it, is capable of discerning whatever can be seen, heard, or otherwise known by the physical senses—plus, of course, its own world of purely astral perceptions.

This means a lot of good things.

## Astral well-being for everyone

To begin with, it means people who are physically deaf, or near-sighted, or have any other bodily disability whether slight or serious, need not carry over that disability into their astral experience.

This needs to be stated emphatically: sometimes, from sheer force of habit, people go on assuming they have this or that disability even in their astral life, and they can need a fair amount of determination and practice in the astral world to be free of it. When they can do so, however, this naturally adds a lot of joy to their astral traveling—and also, whether the physical disability is lightened or not, the spells of awareness of astral freedom can improve considerably the quality of their earthly life.

This applies even to amputations. Your true astral body is whole, fit, and strong; it is a body of light and energy.

Certainly in your astral travels you may meet with lame people, people with scars, and so on. That probably means they still have to realize they are truly free and independent of all bodily mishaps. But it can also be that they've come to regard these blemishes as signs and features of identity, and would not travel without them.

Still, you should always remember that in the astral world no one is bound to any physical limitation whatsoever.

## Thrilling!

This all pervasive, high-level perceptiveness and sensitivity of astral substance confers other benefits, too, upon the traveler. All experiences are enhanced, not only because they are liberated from the possibly dulling effects of earthly sense organs, but also because your perceptions are not limited to definite sense organs at all.

If you hear astral music for instance—and there is incredibly enchanting astral music to be heard—you will not simply receive it with perfect astral ears. You may concentrate upon hearing it with your ears because that's the way you are accustomed to hearing things, but in reality you will be hearing it with all the substance of your astral vehicle.

Similarly with the astral perfumes, delicate yet wonderfully refreshing, which psychic people try in vain to describe in terms of earthly flowers; and a part of their invigorating power lies in the fact that they are not merely inhaled, your entire astral substance is receptive to them.

And so with all else, subject only to your will and attention.

# 2

# Cosmos and Psyche

*Four levels of the universe • The Neo-Platonist View*
*• The material, astral, mental, and spiritual worlds*
*• Our participation in the worlds*
*• Levels of the psyche involved in projection*

O ur universe in its entirety is, in western esoteric thought, discerned as being made up of four "worlds" or levels of being. In ascending order, these four levels of existence are:

- The material world.
- The astral plane.
- The mental realm.
- The spiritual dimension.

The great Neo-Platonist Plotinus (A.D. 203–269) defined these levels as:

- The world of matter.
- The lower soul-world, the actual "soul of the material universe," that looks downward to matter.
- The higher soul-world, that looks upward to Nous.

- Nous: the condition of being that is eternal blessedness, the World of the "Ideas."

## Quality of existence

Much could be discussed as to whether we should consider these levels of being as rigidly separate from each other or as interpenetrating. The important point here is that whether separated or not, these four levels are distinguished one from another by the quality of existence that they support, and by the degree of simplicity or otherwise that is made manifest in them.

## The material world

The material world is of a virtually indescribable complexity. It comprises the entire material universe: our planet earth, our solar system, and all the boundless seething marvel of other suns and systems, galaxies, nebulae, and the rest that lies beyond: all that can be humanly discerned and certainly much more. This material universe has, too, its own nonmaterial forces and currents, its own divine governance and ordering. A boundary between the material and astral worlds is impossible to define, both receiving their vital influences from the higher worlds.

## The astral plane

The next level in ascending order, the astral world, may not seem to those who visit it in perception to be much more simple, but as an essential difference it lacks the dependence upon physical and chemical conditions that governs the material universe, while the influences of such factors as time and distance are much more fluid than they are on the material plane. Both the density and complexity of the astral world are considerably greater than those of the world of mind. However, each of these worlds has within its compass different qualities of existence and of life. Just as the higher reaches of the world of mind are so flooded with the inspiration and ecstasy of the divine light as to seem to the aspiring visionary to be divine in themselves, so the higher levels of the astral world are filled with a beauty and truth so elevated that the psyche, responding to them, can scarcely recognize its joy as a merely natural human emotion.

The astral world is also "the world behind this world," where images of past and present merge with images of the future that is to be and of the future that may perhaps be. It is the world of powerful creative imagination and also of most false delusion, a perilous but indispensable field of action for the occultist. It is the abode of countless hosts of nature spirits: elementals of the most diverse kinds. In its grossest levels, to which human consciousness does not normally find entrance, it is the abode of demonic beings, destroyers. It is also the region of the great undifferentiated stream of astral life, from which ephemeral beings arise continually and to which they continually return, and from the sparkling current of which we embodied beings can also draw new vitality.

## The mental realm

Above the astral world is the world of mind. At this level the simplicity and purity of existence is already so great as to go almost beyond the scope of earthly language. Although mind is still finite, it does not travel but is where it posits itself. It does not think in words, but may find words for what it needs to express—or it may find symbolic formulae, visual, sonic, or other. Such symbols are but the tools of mind, they are not of its nature. It is not, as truly experienced, the world of the plodding processes of logic, induction, and deduction; but of mind in its fullness, luminous, swifter than light.

## The spiritual dimension

Of the spiritual world, the dimension of Godhead, nothing is spoken save in terms of a *Love* which is all-consuming and all-creating, of a

*Life* in which being and action are one, and of a *Light* whose brilliance defeats all discerning; withal, of an incomparable bliss. This world in its entirety can be defined as the Supreme Being: God. But when we say "God is One," it is to be understood that the "One" is truly an entire world, that is to say an entire universe—perhaps many universes of intense spiritual existence-action, beyond the power of any human mind to comprehend. The entire spiritual world is of the divine nature, that is to say, it is wholly divine, it is God; but in discussing various aspects of the spiritual world we often refer to "the divine nature" or the "divine mind." All, however, is one divine reality.

## The human psyche and the worlds

If we consider these four worlds in descending order, each imparts life to that which is below it, with a consequent increase in complexity and decrease in vitality with the greater removal from the Source. At the same time it is true that each world has its own rightful and necessary part in the Great Plan of existence, and each has its own character, beauty, and sublimity.

What, then, of our own nature?

Each individual person participates, while in this present earthly life, in each and all of these four worlds; that is a truth unaffected by a person's degree of conscious awareness of that participation, or any other factor. This means not only that we are a part of the worlds; it means, too, that the nature of each of the worlds is present in each individual person.

## Living relationships

The physical body is one in nature and fabric with the material world. It is sustained by material food; it needs to breathe this earthly atmosphere.

In the psyche the astral level is one in nature with the astral world. Just as the physical body is nourished by the constituents of the material world, so the astral body—the *astrosome*—which comprises the instinctive, emotional and imaginative functions of the person, is nourished and influenced by the tides and currents, the images and impressions of the astral world.

In the hidden life of the cell, gland, and nerve, the action of the astral body and the physical body are inseparably, we may say *indistinguishably*, mingled. There are other activities of the astral body, however, that are almost equally mysterious. Here belong the endless histories of our dream life, both of the sleeping and the wakeful hours. Here originate also those high emotions that border closely upon the world of mind; here, too, the creative impulses of art and science, in whose fulfillment not only the imagination but also the work of the brain and that of the directing mind must take part.

Corresponding to the world of mind is the mental level—the mental sheath or *noemasome*—of the individual person. While all functions of the psyche are necessary to the well-being of the person, those of the mental level have a deep and special importance. Most conspicuous among them is the rational mind, which is concerned not only with thought in the abstract, but with keeping in harmony and "within reason," as we say, the activity of the physical body and of the astral body so that these may each have their own healthy life and expression without taking the rightful place of the higher faculties. This may seem to make an arduous business of living, but in fact rationality is only one of the functions of the mental level of the psyche. Its other function is concerned with the higher faculties themselves: perception of, and receptivity to, high spiritual influences from the spiritual world. The mental level, nourished and strengthened certainly by contacts with the mind-stuff of its own proper habitation, the mental world, has a special receptivity, necessary for its own right balance and for that of the whole person, to these spiritual influences that are of truly divine origin. Delicate at first, with developing awareness they form a strong bond, producing the fully integrated person.

These high influences do not come from a source alien to the individual. On the contrary, they come from the very essence, the inmost spiritual selfhood of a person's being, which resides ever in the spiritual world. That inmost selfhood is a part of the spiritual world, as much one with the divine nature as the physical body is one with the world of earth, air, fire, and water.

To make this plain, we can classify these relationships as follows:

- The physical body, native to the material world.

- The astral body, the astrosome, native to the astral world. The emotional and instinctual level of the psyche, the true seat of the psychic faculties.

- The mental sheath, the noemasome, native to the mental world. The domain of consciousness. The intellect that soars beyond the mechanical processes of the brain, its instrument. The level of the psyche that works with, and controls, the astrosome, while being itself receptive to the influence of the higher faculties of the spiritual self.

- The spiritual self, the abode of the higher faculties, native to the spiritual world. The highest, inmost, level of the psyche, responsible for directing the uplifted mind and for filling it, as it may be prepared, with inspired and ecstatic perception.

## Which levels of the psyche are involved in projection?

In fully willed astral projection your consciousness, the *thinking you,* goes forth from the body. In doing so it draws from the astral body, or you send forth, a certain amount of astral substance through which it will function on the astral plane. This astral substance forms your *light-envelope* or *body of light,* and is the vehicle in which you will travel and through which you will gather information.

Effectively, therefore, the astral body and the mental sheath are the levels of the psyche involved in willed astral projection; that is to say, are involved in the deliberate process whereby you, functioning in and through your body of light, gain awareness of the astral plane and are enabled to function thereon as a fully conscious being.

Just as the consciousness, while functioning through the physical body, has awareness of the material world and is generally aware of the inner worlds only in exceptional circumstances or through the application of special spiritual techniques, so, too, it will ordinarily have awareness of the astral plane (and, to an extent, of the material world), but not of the mental realm, when faring forth in the body of light. Awareness of the mental world depends upon the personal evolution of the individual, and involves the awakening of the full potential of the mind under the influence of the higher faculties.

When astral substance is deliberately sent forth, but the consciousness does not travel with it—as in various techniques to be illustrated later in this book—the operation is under the control of the conscious mind, but only the substance of the astral body is actually involved in projection.

When, as may happen during sleep, a projection of astral substance is involuntarily produced, and the consciousness does not accompany it as it travels forth, the astral body is involved but without the direction of the mental sheath.

As may be seen from the foregoing, therefore, astral projection can range from the nonvolitional type, involving only projection of the substance of the astral body, to the fully willed operation involving both projection of the substance of the astral body and the sending forth of the consciousness.

# 3

# Physical and Astral Preparations

*Choosing a place for astral work • Correct posture
• Sending special signals to the self • Some helpful
factors • Good breathing: a vital condition
• Astral preparation of the place
• Setting apart of the place
• Awakening the Light • Establishing the circle*

First, a few preliminary suggestions as to place, posture, and breathing are made here. You may wonder why, considering how often we hear of people performing various psychic activities without troubling about any such matters, quite naturally and even unaware.

The reason is that now you will want what you do to be more than a lucky accident. You want to reach a point where you can be reasonably sure of the outcome of your actions and intentions. At the same time, the suggestions that will be made are only suggestions. They may not fit in with your ideas, or with your circumstances. In either case, you'll be quite right to change them, adapt them, or just plain ignore them. Do read them, though, and see the reason why each suggestion is made. You may wish to achieve the same purpose some other way.

## Choosing a place

Certainly you need a place and time where you will not be disturbed. Ideally, you should be able to have dim lighting there, and ideally you should be able to sit looking across an empty area in a room, or along a hallway, into deep shadow or toward a dark surface such as a door.

This is because at first you may find astral substance as tricky to see as threads of gossamer, and you'll want to give yourself every chance. A dark screen or curtain, however, can serve your purpose equally well.

Use what you have.

Again: you'll need a space to project astral substance into, and you'll find it easier if you have a real space. When you are expert, you'll know you can project astral substance with full confidence straight through a brick wall; but as a beginner you will find a space more inviting.

## Correct posture

A chair will be required for your astral workings, and this should be a simple, straight-backed piece of furniture on which you can sit comfortably with upright spine.

A bed, or a mattress—a futon, or whatever—will likewise be required, and this should be placed on a north-south axis.

In no circumstances, whether seated or lying down, should your posture involve crossing your arms or your legs. The aim in this is to keep your entire being, in psyche and body alike, free from any real or suggested barrier that might impede the energies that should flow both within you and from the cosmos.

## Signals to yourself

If from the beginning you can keep to the same place, chair, time, everything else, for every activity connected with the astral, this will be a good signal to all the levels of yourself to turn your attention wholly to those matters. But in this, too, should this kind of regular procedure be impossible to you, you may find some other means of giving your whole self a signal, such as these suggestions below.

- Listen to a particular piece of music, something restful, haunting but not too emotive.

- Have a special fragrance where you can smell it. Something simple is best. Jasmine oil has traditional associations with astral activity.

- Sound a small bell. Or keep a particular garment for these occasions: something loose fitting, like a caftan. If you can be nude, better still; but whatever else, take your shoes off!

## Helpful factors

These helpful factors should be noted, as you will be using them in further procedures:

- Uncomplicated posture, straight spine.

- Deep, ample breathing.

- Attention focused upon astral activity.

Whether for a particular plan of action you are standing, seated, or lying down, in light or darkness, silently or with accompanying sounds, these three factors will remain constant and helpful conditions. It is these, too, that your whole nature will come to recognize as standard conditions for whatever astral activity you wish to undertake.

## Vital breathing

Good breathing is not only integral to the mien and deportment of the astral practitioner, it is vital to the right action and power of astral working. If it has been given due attention in the early days of development—and, later, put aside from consciousness as a lesson well learned—it will do much to advance the growth of the astral personality.

What is needed is breathing from the diaphragm. Standing, seated or lying, in the posture of a person who is wide awake, alert, but relaxed, one should imitate the breathing, deep and unhurried, of one who is soundly sleeping.

In learning to breathe well, it is easier and more natural to imitate a sleeping person than to involve one' attention in counting heart beats, or seconds, as is frequently recommended. There exists, furthermore, a strong psychophysical reason for following in this respect the example of the peaceful sleeper.

## Hypnotist and astral practitioner

When a hypnotist wishes to detach someone from the turmoil of the discursive intellect, so as to open that person's mind to subsequent suggestions, his or her first act is to throw the subject into a special state of sleep, which nonetheless permits of any speech and action required. Here, where the astral practitioner is employing this technique of breathing, there is no hypnotist; neither does the subject lie down in the state of passive relaxation which a hypnotist would seek to induce. We have an astral operator who is awake, alert, and in command of his or her own will. Nonetheless, the manner of breathing that, from birth, we have all habitually adopted during sleep has an intensely calming and pacifying influence upon the nervous system and thence upon the lower psyche which is so closely linked to the bodily organism. In this case however it is the astral practitioner's own will, fully awake, and indeed fortified by the absence of distractions, which has the direction of the actions, the faculties, and the emotions of his or her whole lower self.

## The astral preparation of the place

We pass now to some practical considerations concerning the astral preparation of the space of working.

The area of working that you establish may be permanent in nature: your bedroom, say, or a spare room you are able to devote to your astral practices. Or it may be a room that you need to share with a partner or a friend, and that is consequently available to you for your astral workings only on special occasions or even on an irregular basis.

Whatever the circumstances, this room should be *set apart* by you on every occasion of its use in relation to your astral program.

The method of *setting apart* that follows involves, first, the awakening of high spiritual energy and, second, by virtue of that energy, the creation of an astral barrier designed to protect your chosen space from unwanted astral influences and from any astral beings that might happen to be drawn by your activities or by the psychic forces you raise in your work.

This will not, of course, prevent you yourself from astrally leaving the set-apart working area or from sending astral substance beyond the confines of the barrier you have erected.

## Setting Apart of the Place
### Section A
### Awakening the Light

1. Stand in the center of your room, facing east.

2. Turn your attention to the high and primal source of Light and Life, in whatever mode you readily conceive of this. Contemplate it and aspire to it.

   *To direct the attention in this way is a necessary and deliberate act, so that your subsequent contemplation shall also be clear and specific, avoiding a vague dreamy state of confused emotions.*

   *The object of your contemplation is the cosmic fountain of all goodness, beauty, and truth; it is the boundless energy that sustains the worlds; it is the love that moves the sun and all the stars. When you direct your attention upward in this contemplation, you can naturally become aware of a great happiness and peace.*

*You should foster this awareness so that it will increase progressively with your experience of this technique: this will allow your whole being, body as well as soul, to bathe itself in, to savor increasingly, the ambient blessing, the divine influence of that which you contemplate. The happiness and peace thus engendered is genuine, and to be savored as such: it is the natural condition of your psyche in its rightful relationships, free from constraints.*

*To contemplate the supreme source of Light and Life—the ultimate source of your psyche itself—is naturally to be moved to aspiration thereto: an emotion that needs only to receive recognition and encouragement, and which, together with the happiness and peace of your contemplation, will increase strongly with habitude.*

3. Now, in this aspiration, in a mighty and continual reaching upward and outward, imagine yourself growing in stature, steadily increasing in magnitude, becoming vast, immeasurably vast.

   *This is an essential and distinctive step of this formulation: the willed imagination of your whole self, growing in immensity, upward and outward.*

   *An immense psychological benefit resulting from this expansion is the revelation to your consciousness of the great dignity and power inherent in your total selfhood, irrespective of any limitations or conditioning imposed by the circumstances of mundane life.*

4. Maintaining the sense of immensity, formulate imaginatively a globe of brilliant white light just above, but not touching, your head.

   *This globe of light represents, and awakens the energies of, the crown chakra of your astral body. It symbolizes, too, that level of the psyche that is the supreme nexus between your individual personality and the glorious infinity of the divine mind. There is, nonetheless, a safeguard here against any possible danger that this stage of the formulation might lead to a false inflation of the ordinary consciousness, with an appropriation to itself of powers that do not belong inher-*

*ently to it. The sphere of light is located just above, but not touching, the crown of the head. This separation is to denote that the crown chakra, representing the higher self, the link with the divine life, is always above the level of ordinary conscious personality, though the latter should ever aspire to participate in its gifts and should in truth participate increasingly in them, though they are beyond the intrinsic functioning of the rational mind.*

5.  In the realization of this globe, and of the marvel and mystery it implies, visualize its luminosity increasing to an intense radiance that falls upon you and through you, permeates your whole being and surrounds you as an aura of white brilliance.

    *The steady increase of the luminosity of the globe of light, and of the encompassing and permeating brilliance that emanates from it, is not simply an exercise of the visual imagination. To begin to fulfill this phase of the technique aright, the conceptual and emotional imagination must from the outset be engaged with the spiritual beauty and awe-inspiring wonder of the mystery that it represents, transcendent yet intimately present to you. And in the final stages of this visualization you should imagine your whole being as pervaded and aureoled by the glorious light of your divine higher self: a splendor in which even your instinctual and material levels are encompassed.*

### Section B
### Establishing the Circle

6.  Continuing to imagine the globe of light above your head, and the aura of white brilliance that surrounds you, now visualize a circular wall of white light slowly revolving counterclockwise about your room. When you have this clearly in mind, say:

    *BY THE POWER OF THE DIVINE LIGHT OF MY HIGHER SELF, BE THIS PLACE FREE FROM ALL HINDRANCES AND FROM EVERY SHADOW OF DOUBT AND ILLUSION.*

7. Still maintaining the mental image of the globe of light and the en-
compassing aura of brilliance, now visualize a second wall of light,
just within the first. This one, however, should be seen as pale blue
and as revolving clockwise. When you have formulated this, say:

*BY THE POWER OF THE DIVINE LIGHT OF MY
HIGHER SELF, BE THIS PLACE FILLED WITH
PEACE AND WITH THE BLESSINGS OF LOVE
AND GOODNESS*

8. Allow the visualizations to fade from your awareness.

## *Awakening the Light*

The above procedure, then, is in two sections, the first of which—A—
is a powerful and beneficial technique in its own right. We shall meet
with it again, later in this book. For ease of reference and for practical
application, it may be noted that the salient points of the first section
of the *Setting apart of the place* are:

### *Awakening the Light*

1. A standing posture is adopted, facing east.

2. The attention is turned to the source of Light and Life.

3. An imaginative increase of stature is accomplished.

4. The sense of immensity being maintained, a globe of brilliant white
light is formulated just above the head.

5. The luminosity of the globe increases, permeates your entire being,
and surrounds you with an aura of light.

### *Establishing the Circle*

The second section of *Setting apart of the place* involves the creation of
the circle of protection, the establishment of a dedicated space in

In the form of *Setting apart of the place* given here, two circles are constructed: the first, which revolves counterclockwise, is a banishing circle, and when you imaginatively construct it you should hold in mind the intention of cleansing the place of all unwanted astral influences. The second circle, which revolves clockwise, is an invoking circle, and when you formulate this you should hold in mind the intention of filling the defined space with positive vibrations of love, peace, and spiritual energy.

### An ensign of power

As an alternative to forming the second circle, you could instead, after visualizing the first, counterclockwise circle and uttering the affirmation, trace a sign toward each quarter in turn: east, south, west, and north respectively (so as to initiate the clockwise current of invocation). This sign should be something meaningful to you, something in which you wholeheartedly believe, something that signifies to you, personally, the power of spiritual goodness and authority: a cross, for example, or a circled cross; a five-pointed star, or the Star of David, or whatever. To conclude the procedure, when you have completed the tracing of this sign toward the quarters you should utter the second affirmation while facing east.

# 4

# Exciting and Refining
# the Astral Body

*Relationship of the unconscious to the conscious
personality • The flow of life-energies
• Interaction of the levels of the psyche
• Foundation technique
• The immeasurable power of the psyche*

The lower unconscious, in which the astral body is steeped to a greater or lesser extent in everyone, has been considerably explored in the researches of clinical psychology. Similarly the higher unconscious, the "Higher Self" of a person, has been deeply penetrated and analyzed by mystical researchers of the great religious and philosophic schools. Interestingly, many of the findings of the mystics are closely paralleled in the case histories and interpretations given by C. G. Jung in his books. All these matters can be followed out extensively in the appropriate works, but theoretical study is only part—and for our present purpose not the most important part—of the needed activity. *The higher and lower unconscious are the most spiritually potent areas of the psyche; but the rational consciousness must be brought into contact with*

25

*them, so as to direct the lower effectively and to work in harmony with the higher.* It is necessary therefore to bring both these areas as fully as possible into relationship with your conscious personality, without rationalizing them in a way that would nullify their power. It is also for every reason good for your psychophysical well-being to bring a free interaction of the flow of life-energies, both spiritual and instinctual, to your personality in all its levels. This free interaction is needed, apart from its general psychosomatic benefits, to maximize the awareness both inward and cosmic that you can bring into your astral activity.

## Communication of levels

A living basis for this interaction exists already in the structure of the psyche itself. A large number of people who have not yet formed an established communication with their Higher Self certainly possess, from birth or by training, a high degree of psychic perception—perception of forms and emotions in the Astral World directly through their astral body—on which in their daily life they can depend for frequent insight and guidance. There are however other people who have no such familiar doorway into astral perceptions, but who nevertheless in some moment of urgent crisis have received from their inner consciousness a coherent and succinct message, which deals at once and effectively with the matter. Many instances of this isolated but vital communication from the unconscious have been known, such messages being generally remarkable for the cogency and the accuracy of their information, as well as for their brevity and their tone of high authority. The explanation is that because of the seriousness of the crisis—often a matter of life and death—a subliminal channel of communication is opened between the Higher Self and the instinctual level of the psyche: the Higher Self intervening to preserve the wholeness, or even the continued existence, of the incarnate personality which, in most perfect and primal bonding, it entirely loves.

Even apart from interventions of this kind, however, it is essential to the good functioning of your whole personality that each of its levels, the spiritual and the mental as well as the emotional and instinctual, should flow freely into its adjacent levels.

The following simple technique serves two purposes, both very relevant to astral projection. You will feel the benefits of this technique increasingly with use, not only as regards astral practice but also in relation to the whole of your lifestyle. In the first place, it steps up the energy levels of the astral body and ensures free flow of vitality—and, consequently, enhances communication between the levels of the psyche; and in the second place it circulates and redistributes astral energies so that when astral substance is used it is not simply drawn from the "gross astral" level.

## *Foundation Technique*

1. Assume a well-balanced standing posture in which your feet are together and your arms are held loosely at your sides.

2. Maintaining this posture, visualize a sphere of brilliant white light—your crown center—just above your head.

3. On an in-breath, imagine a beam of white light being drawn down from the crown center to your breast, where it forms your heart center as a brilliant white globe.

4. On an out-breath, imagine the beam of white light descending from your heart center to your feet, where it forms another center in white light, radiant but less brilliant than the crown.

5. On an in-breath, see a flash of golden light rise from your feet center and pass upward into your heart center.

6. On an out-breath, the movement of the light rests, and you mentally affirm the three centers and their connecting shaft of white light.

7. Now repeat several times Steps 3, 4, 5, and 6 above.

8. Finally, see your heart center emitting a powerful radiance, to encompass you in an aura of golden light.

This technique should be performed daily, even when you are not specifically pursuing your program of astral activity, and it should always be used immediately before any astral work that you do, in fact, undertake. It should be preceded by the procedure for *Setting apart of the place*.

Even from your first experience of practicing this technique, its good effects will stay with you. They will have penetrated to your bodily awareness and to the unconscious levels of your psyche. With increased practice, as they penetrate more deeply, a greater area of your psyche will be opened to consciousness.

## Widening the horizon

Despite the conventionally accepted norms of possibility, it is a fact that no limits have ever been ascertained for the powers of the psyche at any level of its functioning. Even apart from the spiritual heights, which are inscrutable, the range and power of the mind in its own right—in producing new philosophic and mathematical concepts in response to changed life situations, or in response to the stimulus of new geophysical or astronomical discoveries—is seemingly limitless. So is the unending adventure of astral experience, and so too is the largely unexplored power, sometimes staggering in its visible effects, of the psyche to inhibit or direct seemingly inevitable reactions of the physical body in sickness or in health.

All these manifestations are, however, mere partial indications of the immeasurable intrinsic power of the psyche, a power that is in itself unconditioned, which is greater and more sublime than any of its works perceptible in earthly life. The usual conditions of daily living are as walls that shut out the vast perspectives spiritually and psychically open to each individual. Practice of the *Foundation technique* will help to restore the reality of those perspectives.

The sense of power and joy that will follow from this exercise is not an artificial euphoria. It is the bringing into a degree of awareness, in the interior seclusion of this formulation, of the real vitality and delight that is of the essential nature of your psyche.

# 5

# Fact and Fiction

*Astral projection: a popular study* • *An age-old practice*
• *St. Paul speaks of OBE* • *The astral body in
historical record* • *Blake and Whitman and projection*
• *Robert Benson's Necromancers* • *The Lurker
on the Threshold* • *Lucy Westenra projects*
• *The world behind this one* • *Crystal power*

O ut-of-the-body experience has of late years acquired a
fair amount of recognition in the media, and various
excellent studies and "How To" books exist for the student's
attention. Indeed, so many people are hearing of astral projection, learning about it, practicing it these days, that to
others it may seem either a modern myth—something they
are uncertain whether to believe or not—or a great recent
discovery.

To a great number of people, however, the widespread acceptance of the reality of the experience must come as a
happy reassurance, confirming the actuality of astral episodes
and insights that have taken place in their own lives. And because the subject has been opened up as a legitimate—and
wonderfully exciting—topic for thought and discussion, it's

noticeable how many people will tell in conversation of out-of-the-body recollections they dared not previously expect others to believe, perhaps dared not even fully accept themselves.

But a new discovery it is not.

## In every human culture

Among those with the inner certainty or the warrant of authority to speak for themselves, the out-of-the-body experience has been known and avowed in all regions of the world and through the centuries, in countless variations. Shamans, witch-doctors, ascetics, and mystics in every human culture in Asia and Africa, and across the globe from New Zealand and Australia through the Americas, have always declared and demonstrated their ability to leave the physical body at will, so as to oversee or perform certain actions, or to receive further powers from spiritual levels.

In a famous passage in the second letter to the Corinthians (2 Corinthians, XII, 1-4), the Apostle Paul says:

> *(1) Doubtless it is not fitting for me to glory. I will come to visions and revelations of the Lord. (2) More than fourteen years ago I knew a man in Christ—whether in the body or out of the body I cannot tell, God knows— who was taken up to the Third Heaven. (3) I knew such a man—whether in the body or out of it I cannot tell, God knows— (4) who was caught up into Paradise and heard unspeakable words, not appropriate for anyone to utter.*

To look into ancient records—including biblical records—for hints of projection of consciousness can be fascinating but is not very conclusive. Ancient writings, or records made later from word-of-mouth traditions, were in the first place made for people who already knew the story or at least the mode of thought involved. And ancient languages—as many languages even today—had only a comparatively simple stock of words. So you need to know what is likely to be meant literally and what is likely to be a figure of speech or perhaps, in some cases, a taking for granted of something we moderns, with cautious accuracy, would want expressed in detail. But it seems certain here that Paul (who is certainly speaking of himself) is relating an experience either of separation of body and soul, or of mystical ekstasis in which his consciousness was literally *lifted* beyond the confines of his rational perception.

## The astral body in historical record

It is frequently considered that the concept of "the astral body" is of oriental origin, but speculation concerning the astral body and its powers has a long history in western thought and reaches back into classical Greece, to the writings of Plato and Aristotle. Plotinus, Porphyry, Iamblichus, Proclus, and others great thinkers of the Neo-Platonic tradition, have all added in their turn to the measure of our understanding of the phenomenon. Macrobius, in the late fourth century A.D., speaks of the "putting on of the luminous body" in his commentary on the *Dream of Scipio*, and Boethius (480–524) writes of the "rising chariot" in his *Consolation of Philosophy*. Consideration of the subject pervades the thought of medieval Europe; and the Hermetic societies of the Middle Ages and the Renaissance, aligning their studies with those of the Qabalistic tradition, brought other vital aspects of the tradition of the body of light into the scheme. In the seventeenth century of our era the scholar Ralph Cudworth included a study of it in his *Intellectual System*. In the nineteenth and twentieth centuries the work of western occultists, and of occult societies, added greatly by way of technique and understanding to the depth and range of the study.

So we need not look to an oriental source for the body of light and its powers—the great Hindu treatises on the subtle body, for example, representing a parallel research and garnering of knowledge concerning the human psyche—although it should be noted that quite early in its development the doctrine, as set forth by the neo-Platonists, was influenced by the astral mysticism of Babylonia.

## Two pioneers in poetry

Poets are not always the most explicit of writers, but two remarkable poets should be noted here for their part in the growing plainness of expression regarding out-of-the-body experience.

William Blake (1757–1827) mentions in his *Songs of Innocence* a going out through "the door in the crown of the head." That is truly one of the regions of the body at which astral substance can be sent out to build up a vehicle, and the consciousness as a result can go forth at that point; but it is not one of the easiest regions to use, and people on record as using it for astral perception or travel are, on the whole, people of advanced spiritual development.

Walt Whitman (1819–1892) in his poem *The Sleepers* gives a whole recognizable account of an out-of-the-body experience, although, not surprisingly, with no concern as to the details of achieving that state. It could just be a work of imagination; but to the reader experienced in astral travel or in accounts of astral travel, *The Sleepers* has rather too many convincing touches for fantasy.

## Benson's Necromancers

Robert Hugh Benson (1871–1914), the son of an archbishop of Canterbury and who became a priest in the Church of Rome, was a talented novelist. He evidently researched his subject matter with care, but slanted his writings to purposes of religious propaganda. One of his novels, *The Necromancers*, belongs, to judge by the costume of the characters, to the later years of the nineteenth century. Its main subject is Spiritualism, and despite the author's manifest bias some of the descriptions of phenomena are very fine, vivid, and undoubtedly based on reality.

The hero of the story, however, his psychic faculties awakened by his growing interest in nonmaterial activity, himself experiences a first out-of-the-body trip which, naturally, puzzles him. Having nobody else he can ask about it, he asks a Spiritualist medium, who can't tell him much except that these things happen.

Now the author's prejudice comes into play. The young man in the story asks the fairly usual question, "What if I didn't get back?"

"Then you would not get back," replies the other.

## With intent to frighten

Now this, of course, is intended to frighten the reader and to give the idea that psychic endeavor is dangerous. Its reasoning is as trivial as if a person, asking some absurd thing such as, "What if the sky should fall?" were to be answered, "In that case, the sky would fall!"—without any regard for fact. The reply in the novel probably did frighten many who were reading it because they were interested in psychic development. It probably influenced other writers, too, since the passage also contains reference to that much-misunderstood bogey, "the Lurker on the Threshold."

## A monster deflated

There would be no excuse for introducing this outworn topic here, except if you collect books on astral projection you may chance to find it in some older ones. The idea is, if you get out of your body, when you want to return you'll encounter some monstrous image, phantom, or feeling of horror which will try to keep you out.

None of the modern books mention this, because they are based on real experience, and nobody ever meets such a monster. The truth, as you'll soon find, is just the opposite: when you first get out of your body, the chief difficulty is to keep yourself from being attracted straight back in!

## The real "Lurker"

The real "Lurker on the Threshold" is a quite different thing, and is not at all specifically related to astral projection.

You may never experience it. If you have a friend who does, however, you'll need a great combination of sympathy, encouragement, and firm determination to help fight it.

The problem is this. When some people decide to set themselves a program of any kind of inner development, they find themselves met at the beginning by some crushing negative influence. It may be anything from a feeling of horror to a simple inability to *get going,* or even a recurring doubt as to whether they really want to do it. Fear of failure is another apparent reason for not beginning. The underlying causes of the trouble are, usually, any or all of the following:

- Fear of the unknown.

- An irrational and perhaps unformulated sense of guilt or unworthiness.

- The ever-present human aversion to making an effort.

These three factors, in whatever proportions, make up the "Lurker" which would keep us from all progress.

## Bram Stoker's Dracula

First published in 1897, *Dracula,* Bram Stoker's classic of occult fiction, was written with no purpose but to grip and thrill the reader and, in fact to meet a challenge as to Stoker's ability to write a novel about vampires.

It contains, however, the fruits of extensive research; and although at some points both history and tradition have naturally been bent to the purposes of the storyteller's art, yet much material incidentally introduced is plainly based on real-life facts.

The following excerpt is from Lucy Westenra's story of her first encounter with Dracula, when she went from sleepwalking into a deeper trance state in which her consciousness left her body. She speaks to her friend Mina:

> . . . *and then everything seemed passing away from me;*
> *my soul seemed to go out from my body and float about*
> *in the air. I seem to remember that once the West Light-*

*house was right under me, and then there was a sort of*
*agonizing feeling, as if I were in an earthquake, and I*
*came back and found you shaking my body. I saw you be-*
*fore I felt you.*

That is, recognizably, the well-observed experience of someone whose consciousness has temporarily separated from the physical body through a special occurrence. Mina panicked, and with some effort shook Lucy's body back into wakefulness; Lucy describes her consciousness being violently brought back, and how, in the instant before re-entering the body, she astrally observed the action of her friend. Next moment, the shaking is felt "from within" as a normally awakening person would feel it.

As fiction, Bram Stoker's masterpiece became at once and lastingly popular. Had he published his factual researches—even the mildest of them—as truth, however, he might have found himself disastrously ahead of what the public at large would have been willing to see in print.

## Oglala Sioux

Thirty years into the twentieth century, a remarkable book of true experiences entered upon its long and hard road to fame.

*Black Elk Speaks*, by John G. Neihardt, was first published in 1932. In it the author transcribes what was told him by Black Elk, a holy man of the Oglala Sioux. Some notable visions and astral experiences, both of Black Elk himself and of others, are recorded, but the decade was too early for the frank acceptance of these and probably, too, for the serious presentation of Native American history and ways of thought.

Not until 1961, when in some ways the general viewpoint had been very considerably transformed, was the book reprinted (currently available editions: University of Nebraska Press, 1979–2001). Then, however, it swiftly gained the recognition it deserved, and has become a landmark in its own subject area.

# The world behind this one

It is not only the astral experiences themselves that interest us here, nor even the acceptance of them as a normal part of life, but also the Native American's explanation of their nature: for it is just the same explanation as that given in Egypt and eastern Mediterranean lands many centuries back.

Black Elk tells, for example, of a vision which his cousin, the famous warrior Crazy Horse, had as a boy. Black Elk begins by saying that in a dream the boy went into the world *behind* the material world, the world whose cast shadows we see in the material world. This ancient and widespread view of the astral world is based on the perception that many happenings and changes there precede, and in some cases plainly bring about, similar happenings and changes at the material level.

At the same time, it may encourage some aspiring seers to note that a young Sioux warrior was not instantly an expert in etheric seeing. In this vision the boy was riding his horse but, not being accustomed to astral seeing, he got an impression of everything shimmering like moving water:

> *His horse was standing still there, and yet it danced*
> *around like a horse made only of shadow, and that is*
> *how he got his name . . .*

# Between soul-power and
# science: the crystal

We turn from the traditions of the past to the dreams of the future.

The fact that certain people are able—that certain people have always been able—to project their conscious presence at will into other places and other times, is a knowledge that haunts the imagination of humanity, telling our submerged awareness that we should all be able to utilize this power, given the right conditions.

And the right conditions, always, include enough energy and the means to channel it to the desired purpose.

Given those requirements, we are free to travel all the worlds.

"You can't really think a man's mind could leave his body and go starfaring?"

"I do think it," she said.

That is a quotation from Edmond Hamilton's *Starwolf* (Ace Books, 1982), an epic of Space Age science fiction. The people in that story achieve out-of-the-body consciousness without practice, and in some cases without intention, through a mighty energy that infuses their brain from the emanations of a huge, scientifically organized mass of crystals.

That is a thinkable theory, although present-day science has, perhaps fortunately, not progressed so far. The main difficulty is that the ordinary human consciousness, if it is in fact to *be* conscious, does need a vehicle of some kind through which to be aware of its surroundings; and the level of the psyche that can cause the formation of such a vehicle is controlled, not through the cerebro-spinal system but through the autonomic ones.

Given its use in relation to the heart and solar plexus instead of the brain, therefore, to bring in crystal power as an aid to stimulate the energies for astral projection is an altogether valid device. Most people are innately attracted by the light that is mysteriously gathered and given forth by crystals and gemstones, and the potent energies that accompany such radiation have become again, as in ancient times, a subject of deep study.

# 6

# Astral Substance:
# Play and Power

---

*The versatility and potential of your astral body*
*• Free-flowing astral substance*
*• Working with astral substance • The first play*
*• Forming the sphere of light*
*• Directing the astral sphere • Astral threads*
*• Astral messages • Beneficent wishes*
*• Greetings and blessings on the astral*

---

The stuff of your astral body is extremely elastic and variable in density. It ranges from the etheric, near-material ectoplasm so dear to nineteenth-century mediums, to the most delicate refinement of astral vibrations that can move with the speed and subtlety of thought.

In its mid-range of density, astral substance serves for a number of valuable purposes, including the creation of a functional body in which our consciousness can comfortably travel, feel and do. And when you direct it forth, but keep your consciousness in your physical body meanwhile, it is capable of a number of psychic feats, of which psychokinesis is an example.

## Free-flowing astral substance

Sometimes such things as psychokinesis can occur quite without a person's volition. You may have sometimes said, or heard a friend say something like, "I only looked at that card, and it fell off the shelf." To some people, such happenings are almost a commonplace although they have no idea how they do it.

In fact, the astral body does not have a firmly fixed boundary to enclose it as the skin encloses the physical body. Each person has about them a free-flowing quantity of astral substance, the amount varying with health, fitness, and practice, which can be sent forth very easily and even spontaneously.

Astral substance is fun to play with. Even without leaving your physical body you'll become familiar with the reality of astral substance and with its easy accessibility; you'll get the feel of shaping and consciously directing it.

## *The First Play*

1. Commence with the *Setting apart of the place*.

2. Perform the *Foundation technique*.

3. Have a chair on which you can sit comfortably upright. When seated, place your feet evenly on the floor. Make your breathing steady and full, not straining to fill your lungs but as if you were in a deep, peaceful sleep.

4. After settling into this posture and way of breathing, raise your two hands before you so you see them with the dark surface or area of shadow as a background. The palms should be facing each other, close but not touching. Slightly separating the fingers of each hand, bend your fingers and place each fingertip against its opposite: forefinger to forefinger, middle finger to middle finger, and so on; and thumb to thumb.

   Keep your fingertips pressing firmly but not violently against each other, maintain your steady breathing and remain in this position for, say, three minutes as a rough estimate.

5. When you feel you are ready, stop pressing your fingertips together. Slowly and gently draw them back from each other, watching carefully while you do this. You should see a delicate whitish film or thread of astral substance, faintly luminous, stretching from each fingertip to the one you have just parted it from. (The same with the thumbs, of course.)

6. If you do see it, with the same gentle movement see how far you can part your hands, still keeping the delicate film visible. If you don't see it, try again. Deepen your breathing a little, perhaps increase the pressure of the fingertips slightly, extend the time a little. Also, look in a deliberate and contemplative way to see the manifestation of astral substance.

## *Finishing the First Play*

1. At the end of the time you decide upon, make a point of drawing the astral substance back into yourself. Even if you haven't seen any, chances are you have drawn a small amount out of your fingertips. Besides, it could be that you haven't seen it because your etheric vision is undeveloped as yet: that power to see at least the closer-to-earth levels of astral substance, which practically everyone can develop with a little practice and perseverance.

   So, still breathing in the same even rhythm, bring your fingertips together just as gently as you parted them in the first instance. As you breathe in, imagine the astral substance that was drawn out from your fingers being drawn back into your system.

2. Do this for five or six breaths, then gently part your fingers and look. You should see no astral substance; but repeat for four more breaths if necessary.

3. Pass your fingers and palms over each other a few times as if you were smoothing lotion into them.

4. Perform the *Foundation technique.* This effectively concludes the procedure.

## Repeat sessions: the essentials

You should repeat this simple series of actions for a few more sessions. You'll find you are soon able to see the delicate astral film more strongly and distinctly. This will be partly because you are training your natural faculty of etheric vision, but also—with even more importance for your inner development—because you are beginning, by some very simple means, to step up the activity of astral substance in your whole system.

## *Forming the Sphere of Light*

The next step is fun. Besides being a prime secret of astral magick it gives you the key to some truly mysterious actions.

1. Commence with the *Setting apart of the place.*

2. Perform the *Foundation technique.*

3. Be seated, without shoes, in a soft light and facing a dark area. Take up your steady and deep breathing, as if asleep.

4. Raise your hands before you, against the dark background. This time, however, keep the fingers of each hand together and place palm to palm: *the four fingers of your right hand should lie between the thumb and first finger of your left hand, with the right thumb outside the left thumb.* The hands should be comfortably angled, not quite vertical, and not quite horizontal.

   Don't fold the fingers of either hand over the back of the other hand. The reason for this is the same as for the loose garments and the absence of shoes: everything is to encourage free circulation alike of your blood, of your astral substance, and of your energy.

5. Press your palms firmly together and remain thus for a time (say, about three minutes). Be aware that astral substance will be flowing from the center of each palm, where an important point of communication between your astral and physical bodies is located.

6. The vibrations of right and left hand differ reciprocally; the astral substance from each hand becomes charged correspondingly, and

when you gently separate your hands you will see a patch of pale astral substance floating, as it were, midway between the palms. So draw your hands three or four inches apart, keeping your attention upon the small area of pale astral substance. This will become more condensed and distinct; it is likely to be of a slightly warmer color than the pale luminescence you previously brought from your fingertips.

7. Still gazing at the area of astral substance, *will* it to become a perfect sphere. You can separate your palms a little further at this stage. Between them, distinct against the dark background, the astral substance will show as a simple and perfect sphere.

## Yours to command

This ball of astral substance is yours to command. Practice, silently, willing it to move. Try sending it upward about six inches, then bringing it back to its original position.

You may at first need to think in words—"Go up, up!"—"Now come down!"—but with practice you should be able to make it obey your will, just as, for instance, your hand does when you wish to raise it.

Remember, this is a ball of your own astral substance.

It is not even separated from you.

When you have sent it up into the air for a short distance, turn your attention for a moment to the space between it and your hands. If your etheric sight is sharp enough, you can see the fine threads of astral substance still connecting the ball to each of your palms.

Send it up to about twelve inches high and bring it back; then send it about two or three feet. Each time, bring it back: at first to its original position between your palms, then, after a little experience of this, to the fingertips of one hand or the other as you shall decide. Then bring it, via the fingertips, to rest in the palm of left or right hand alone.

## Gentle progress

Again, however well you succeed, don't try to go too far in any one session. Step by step you can gain the ability to direct the ball of astral substance into the right or left palm at will, as soon as you have formulated it; to send it up through the ceiling, or away from you in any direction you will, and back to you. Simply by sustained will and attention, the time needed becoming shorter with practice, you can make it glow with light.

Always throughout each session keep up your special breathing. Always, for these practice sessions, establish your regular signals to yourself.

Always, after you have sent the ball away from yourself, remember to bring it back as promptly as possible.

## *Concluding the Astral Session*

1. Return the ball to its position between your palms.

2. If you have charged it with light or with anything else, give your attention to seeing it, and knowing it to be, free of that charge: restored to its normal faintly luminous state, cool and unconditioned.

3. Very slowly, close your hands over it, placing your fingers as you did in order to produce it, and consciously reabsorb it into your system with a series of several inbreaths.

4. Now pass your fingers and palms over each other a few times as if smoothing lotion into them.

5. Finally, perform the *Foundation technique*.

## Potential of the astral ball: the thread

The most vital part, and the most astonishing part, of the astral ball is at the same time its least conspicuous feature: the *thread* that connects it to your astral body.

There may be a thread from each hand, as we have seen. When you are employing the distinctive energies of left and right hand, these two threads are both kept in action. This is often the case in a healing, when you need to disperse or remove something that impedes the healing, and at the same time to give the sufferer an extra charge of energy to overcome exhaustion or shock, or to make an increased effort for recovery.

Considered in that way, the astral ball is simply functioning as an extension of your hands, to convey the healing powers you could ordinarily transfer through them. The difference is that you can send the astral ball for healing to someone a considerable distance away.

If you do send the ball for a long distance, or if you give a command that involves your whole self rather than the specific powers of left or right, you may all at once notice the ball is attached simply by one thread to your stronger hand, or to your solar plexus. Don't trouble about it!—in fact, even if you completely ignore its existence, the thread will function perfectly well and will continue to keep the ball as a living part of your astral body. (After all, if it hadn't been pointed out to you, you might never have noticed the thread at all.)

Should you want to send the ball through a dense and thorny forest, you can do so just as easily as if it were in no way attached to you. No danger of the thread being caught up in thorns or branches!—this is astral substance, and the ball can go straight to the destination you intend. Its connection remains unbroken and you can recall it when you will.

## The astral ball: further uses

When you have formulated the astral ball between your palms, you can hold it there, look at it, and meanwhile instill a charge into it.

To charge the ball with a message, you do in fact need to *think* the message in words as you sit looking at the ball.

## *Sending an Astral Message*

1. Commence with the *Setting apart of the place*.
2. Perform the *Foundation technique*.

3. Form the astral ball, as described above in *Forming the sphere of light.*

4. Speak the words of your message softly to it, several times.

5. Close your hands over the ball with the fingertips and thumbs of the two hands touching.

6. Raise your joined hands—your hands enclosing the astral ball will at this point make the shape of a pointed bud—and, keeping the thumbs together, part the little fingers so as to open the hands away from you.

7. Blow gently upon the ball.

8. Now form a clear idea of the person for whom the message is intended—and send the ball forth.

9. After a short while—say, about one minute—recall the ball.

10. Perform the steps outlined above in *Concluding the astral session.*

You should by now be able to see the astral ball, at least faintly, by ordinary daylight. Another person however would not be likely to see it unless they were unusually psychic, or unless they were carefully looking for it.

Without using words, you should be able to increase the luminosity of the ball while you cradle it in your palms or keep it suspended about twelve inches above your hands. Your astral body as a whole is very luminous: you have simply to will an extra portion of this light to pass into the ball. It is simple, but may need practice because the ideas are so unfamiliar.

This technique is often used prior to sending a wish for well-being to another person; the intention to increase the luminosity of the ball of astral substance itself assisting with the consequent radiation of blessing.

To send good and positive energy by means of the ball of astral substance can very effectively bestow comfort and inspiration, and even act as a positive catalyst to the recipient's psyche.

To send a wish for well-being, proceed as follows.

# *Sending a Beneficent Wish*

1. Commence with the *Setting apart of the place.*

2. Perform the *Foundation technique.*

3. Form the astral ball, as described in *Forming the sphere of light.*

4. Speak your blessing, your good wishes, to it slowly and softly, once; then will it to become more luminous.

5. Close your hands over the ball, with the fingertips and the thumbs of the two hands touching.

6. Raise your joined hands and, keeping the thumbs together, part the little fingers so as to open the hands away from you.

7. Blow gently upon the ball.

8. Form a clear idea of the person for whom the blessing is intended, their circumstances and their need—and send the ball forth.

9. After a while, say about five minutes, recall the ball.

10. Perform the steps outlined in *Concluding the astral session.*

A useful precaution can be noted. When you have charged the astral ball for any purpose, upon its recall restore the substance to its normal state before you reabsorb it into your system. The charge may have been used up, or it may not.

Although you have brought all the elements out of yourself, they might disorganize you somewhat if they returned into your system in too great a concentration. At any event, it's good to do things properly!

## The astral ball out-of-the-body

Earlier we mentioned that the ball remains connected by its astral thread to your astral body.

An interesting conclusion can be drawn from this, and is, in fact, perfectly true. When you are out of your body, traveling in a body of your astral substance, you will still be able to formulate and send these astral balls, just as in earth-life.

You can charge them with energy and send them as a greeting or a blessing to other beings on the astral.

One more thing may occur to you about these little balls of astral substance. If you could transfer your consciousness into one of them, could you go astral traveling that way?

The answer is, yes, you could; but you are not used to living in a body of those dimensions. You would, for instance, be able to see, hear, smell, feel, but without the familiar orientations and sense of direction given by eyes, ears, and so on. You need to be a thoroughly experienced astral traveler before you set yourself that sort of problem.

# 7

# Opening Channels of
# Communication

---

*The solar plexus and astral activity • A need for
caution • A prelude to fully conscious astral projection
• Solar and lunar cycles • Creating and sending the
Watcher • Recalling and reading the Watcher
• An advanced method of receiving information
• Reading the active Watcher
• Extending the range of operation*

---

The upper abdominal region, the solar plexus, is of considerable significance in astral works. From it, astral substance can be sent forth and formed into a *simulacrum*—an astral double of the self—or formed into a specific image, such as a robed figure, say, or a sphere. This region of the body is also that by which impressions received through a projected simulacrum or image are absorbed, and made available to the reflective and interpretative faculties of the rational consciousness.

## A word of caution

Your experiments with astral substance will have assured your unconscious of your intention to enter into a working relationship with it: a
relationship in which you are the senior partner and are responsible for
setting the pace and directing the program. Your unconscious, remember, is rather like a child: it will take delight in shared endeavors and
will aim to please you, but it needs to know the rules. This is particularly so in relation to astral work, where unchecked activity on the part
of your astral body could result in *astral bleeding*—that is, erratic leak-
age of your astral substance—and consequent production of polter-
geist-type phenomena.

## The Watcher

The following technique, where the above caution must be rigorously
observed, utilizes the solar plexus region of the body for ejection of astral substance, the formation of that substance into an image, and the
sending forth of that image to gather information. This technique is
generally referred to as "creation of a Watcher." It is a development and
use of the powers of the astral body that forms a true prelude to fully
conscious astral projection; but it also forms a valuable procedure in its
own right, a means of collecting impressions, of gathering knowledge
from a distance.

The time of performing this experiment is important. In the first
place, due regard should be directed to the phases of the moon. The
moon controls the tides of the ocean and of the astral plane alike,and
the energies of the astral body are most active and harmonious during
the moon's waxing cycle, so this work should be done during the period from the new moon to the full moon. In the second place, the
solar cycle should be taken into account, for the sun has great influence
upon the rational consciousness; but this influence is weakest during
the period we call "the Dark of the Year"—that is December 21 to
March 21 for the Northern Hemisphere, June 21 to September 22 for
the Southern Hemisphere—and so this period should be avoided for

astral work. By taking these two factors into account—the solar and lunar tides—you ensure that your work is founded in vital astral energy, and that you control it with undiminished strength and reason.

## *Creating and Sending the Watcher*

1. Commence with the *Setting apart of the place.*

2. Perform the *Foundation technique.*

3. From the region of your upper abdomen, imagine astral substance, as a silver-gray stream of light, being sent forth to a distance of about eight feet from your physical body, where it forms a luminous cloud, also of silver-gray light.

4. Now form the cloud into either a robed and hooded figure or into a sphere, composed of silver-gray light. *There is no need to imagine a vast amount of astral substance being ejected in this process.*

5. When you have completed forming the figure, will the ejection of astral substance from your solar plexus to cease. *The figure or sphere you have created will remain connected to you, of course, by the cord of light stretching from it to your abdomen.*

6. Mentally formulate a command to the figure or sphere—for instance ordering it to go to such-and-such a place or person—and then, by an act of will, *send* it to the desired location. *As the figure proceeds away from you, the connecting cord will become thinner and will seem to vanish, although in reality it will still connect you and the Watcher.*

This completes the first part of the technique.

You should now allow the Watcher to go about its business while you go about yours.

After a period of approximately twenty minutes  proceed to the recall of the figure or sphere, as follows:

# *Recalling and Reading the Watcher*

1. Facing the direction in which the Watcher was dispatched, mentally summon the figure or sphere. See it approach to within about eight feet of your physical body. See it as connected to you by the silver cord.

2. Now return the figure or sphere to the form of the luminous silver-gray cloud and reabsorb this through the silver cord, finally reabsorbing the cord itself.

3. Perform the *Foundation technique*, to realign your psychic levels and to ensure proper distribution of the energies you have awakened.

4. Now, seated comfortably, clear your mind of concerns and allow impressions gathered by the Watcher to rise into your consciousness. *At the level of your instincts and emotions, the experiences of the Watcher have become your experiences with your reabsorption of the figure or sphere, and they are now going to rise from your unconscious to your conscious mind where they will be subject to interpretation by you. Remember, the Watcher is composed of astral substance, and it functions without the presence of your guiding consciousness; it can of itself neither reason nor make deductions.*

## Experiencing the flow

A more advanced method of receiving information from the Watcher can be utilized after you have gained familiarity with the primary technique of creating the figure or sphere, sending it forth, and interpreting impressions after its recall and reabsorption.

Once you have attained proficiency in reading the information you are able to retrieve after assimilation of the Watcher, you can proceed to interpret information while the figure or sphere is actually collecting it. Your link with the figure, through the silver cord that connects you to it, will enable you to do this quite easily. Impressions will arise into your consciousness for interpretation by your rational mind as the Watcher goes about its work, and your skill in retrieving information—acquired through your use of the primary technique—will ensure that you are able to keep pace with the experiences of the Watcher.

## *Reading the Active Watcher*

1. Commence with the *Setting apart of the place.*

2. Perform the *Foundation technique.*

3. Create the Watcher, as explained above in sections 2, 3, and 4 of *Creating and sending the Watcher.*

4. Mentally formulate your command, and then by an act of will send the Watcher off on its appointed task.

5. Be seated comfortably. Establish an even breathing rhythm.

6. When you are ready, make a mental resolution to receive the information that is being gathered by the Watcher.

7. Allow impressions to rise into your consciousness, interpreting them as they come into your mind.

8. At the conclusion of your session, stand up, and recall the figure or sphere. See it approach to within about eight feet of your physical body. See the connecting cord that unites you with the Watcher.

9. Return the Watcher to the state of a luminous silver-gray cloud, and reabsorb this through the silver cord. Then reabsorb the cord.

10. Conclude your session with the *Foundation technique.*

## The domain of activity

Generally, the range of application of this practice—whether it involves recalling and reading the Watcher, or whether it involves reading the active Watcher—is restricted to what may be called "present earthly interest." In other words, the Watcher is sent to a locale or to a person in the physical world in order to fulfill its purpose of gathering information. Even so, the Watcher itself functions upon the astral level. It perceives earthly happenings from an inner dimension, spatially and causally removed from the material. It is quite possible, therefore, to extend its range of operation to include higher levels of the Astral World, and to set it to seek out specific knowledge of spiritual beings and astral conditions of the past, present, and future.

In this deeper quest, considerable preliminary meditation upon the task to be set the Watcher, and upon the area of your interest, will need to be undertaken. The command given to the figure or sphere will accordingly need to be specific as to the intended region of the operation and the purpose of your inquiry.

# 8

# Entering the Astral Light

---

*Foundations for success in out-of-the-body experience*
*• Methods of astral projection • A new perspective*
*• Sending astral substance back to the body*
*• The astral cord • Returning to the physical body*
*• Reabsorption of astral substance*

---

Your experiments in working with astral substance are of value to you in two ways. In the first place, your psyche will recognize that you are taking it and its potential quite seriously, and so it will respond all the more readily to any call your rational mind may make upon its astral powers. In the second place, you will now be aware from personal experience of the reality of astral substance, and familiar with sending it forth upon whatever purpose and recalling it.

You are developing, in fact, a relationship of trust and cooperation between your physical, everyday self and your astral body; and in so doing you are laying the foundations for successful adventures in out-of-the-body experience.

The next step is, literally, to step into the astral dimension.

## Astral projection

Four methods are given here by which you can achieve fully conscious and willed astral projection. You may find you prefer one method above the others, and so find yourself using it regularly; or you may like to use the various techniques in turn, one on this occasion, and one on that.

The *Setting apart of the place* being first conducted, each of these methods is preceded by the Foundation Technique, which in this context is to be performed by you while you are lying down; and the chosen form of astral projection in each case is accomplished while you are lying down, nude.

The solar and lunar tides should be taken into account for this work, just as they were for the formulation of a Watcher.

## *Astral Projection Method 1*
### *The stepping forth*

1. Commence with the *Setting apart of the place.*

2. Lying down, perform the *Foundation technique.*

3. Now mentally state your intention to project astrally, using some such affirmation as, "I will go forth into the astral world, now, in full consciousness."

4. Maintaining your awareness of the golden aura that surrounds your physical body, see yourself as wearing, as it were, an image of yourself in silver-gray light—almost like a second skin.

5. Concentrate your attention upon this astral light-envelope that surrounds you: be aware of the silver-gray figure and of the outer aura of golden light.

6. Transfer your awareness into the astral simulacrum of yourself that you have thus formed, so that your awareness of your physical body is lessened and your consciousness of the silver-gray figure and the golden aura is heightened.

7. Now imagine yourself stepping forward, upward, and away from your physical body, in the silver-gray figure. *The effect will be that after you have taken the initial step you will be carried forward, upward, in a gentle gliding motion, and your consciousness will be separated from your body in the achievement of real out-of-the-body experience. You will be aware of the astral simulacrum, the silver-gray light envelope, which will function as your body of light, but you will not be aware of the aura of golden light that surrounded you while you were in your physical body.*

8. Once you have succeeded in making this transition you will not need to continue visualizing the astral simulacrum; though you may wish to strengthen it, to fill in the details, by an act of will. You may at first find, for instance, that your extremities, your fingers and toes, are not as well defined as you would wish; but this is a matter that will actually be better managed by you as you become more practiced in the formulation of your astral body of light prior to projection. Or you may wish to clothe yourself in a manner that you consider appropriate to astral adventure, in which case you simply have to think of yourself as wearing the desired garments. In the early stages, of course, you are likely to discover that you need practice in "tailoring the image," but equally you will soon achieve viable proficiency in the matter.

## *Astral Projection Method 2*
### *Change of perspective*

1. Commence with the *Setting apart of the place.*

2. Lying down, perform the *Foundation technique.*

3. Mentally state your intention to project astrally, using an affirmation such as, "I will go forth into the astral world, now, in full consciousness."

4. Maintaining your awareness of the golden aura that surrounds you, confirm your awareness of your physical body by turning your awareness to it.

5. Remain in this contemplative state for several minutes.

6. Now, transfer your awareness to a point outside your body, say about eight feet above you and facing toward yourself. As you do this, imagine your astral light-envelope coming into being, downward from your point of transferred awareness, so that you are within your body of light and looking toward your physical body.

# *Astral Projection Method 3*
## *The going forth*

1. Commence with the *Setting apart of the place.*

2. Lying down, perform the *Foundation technique.*

3. From the region of your upper abdomen, imagine astral substance, as a silver-gray stream of light, being sent forth to a distance of about eight feet from your physical body, where it forms a luminous cloud, also of silver-gray light.

4. Now form the cloud into a robed and hooded figure, composed of silver-gray light. *As in creating a Watcher, there is no need to imagine a vast amount of astral substance being ejected in this process.*

5. When you have completed forming the figure, *will* the ejection of astral substance from your solar plexus to cease.

6. See the silver-gray figure above you, connected to your abdomen by the cord of silver light. *See the cord connected to the figure's abdominal region as well as to your own.*

7. Maintaining your visualization of this figure, center your awareness in your *point of consciousness,* that is, the special point at which you locate the *thinking* you. For most people this place is the forehead. As you concentrate on this point you will feel a sense of warmth and vitality throughout your body. Then be aware of the corresponding point on the astral figure you have created.

8. Now make a mental resolution to transfer your consciousness into the astral figure above you.

9. Immediately after making this resolution, imagine yourself—gathered as it were at your point of consciousness—gliding swiftly upwards to the astral figure and entering it at the corresponding point of consciousness.

10. And now, orientate yourself to the viewpoint of the astral figure. Mentally turn around, so that you see your physical body lying below you.

11. Feel yourself into the astral figure. Become aware of the body, the hands and the feet of your new astral light-envelope.

# *Astral Projection Method 4*
## *The revolving formula*

1. Commence with the *Setting apart of the place.*

2. Lying down, perform the *Foundation technique.*

3. Mentally state your intention to project astrally, using an affirmation such as, "I will go forth into the astral world, now, in full consciousness."

4. Maintaining your awareness of the golden aura that surrounds your physical body, see yourself as wearing an image of yourself in silver-gray light.

5. Concentrate your attention upon this astral light-envelope that surrounds you: be aware of the silver-gray figure and of the outer aura of golden light.

6. Transfer your awareness into the simulacrum of yourself that you have thus formed, so that your awareness of your physical body is lessened and your consciousness of the astral figure and the surrounding aura is heightened.

7. Now imagine that your astral form, with which your consciousness is identified, begins to revolve within your physical body—slowly at first, and then more rapidly.

8. The motion increases, lessening the hold that your physical body has upon your astral light-envelope. Then, when a steady momentum of movement has been created by you, imagine yourself carried forth to a position above your physical body by the whirling motion.

9. Now cause all movement of your astral light-envelope to cease, so that you are in a position of repose, facing toward your physical body. Orientate yourself to your surroundings, and affirm your awareness of your astral light-envelope.

## Success

In each of these methods for achieving astral projection, actual success in achieving transference of your consciousness to the astral world may be accompanied by a distinct sound, described by those who have experienced it as "a metallic click." This sound is not always heard, and frequently it only occurs on the occasion of a first successful out-of-the-body experience.

For some people, too, the click may be audible when they re-enter their body.

Your attempts to transfer your consciousness to the astral plane may be rewarded with early success; but, equally, you may need to put in considerable work upon the methods of astral projection before you find the freedom of the astral world.

When you do succeed in transferring your consciousness to the astral world by one or other of the methods given here, you will find yourself in a dimension in which there is no apparent light-source, but in which everything is suffused with a pale blue luminescence. You will see yourself lying down, and you will see the room in which your astral experiments are taking place.

## A different perspective

On the first occasion of out-of-the-body experience you should content yourself with the experience of your newfound astral freedom simply.

Resist the temptation to visit a friend, or in fact to travel any great distance from your physical body. You will find the adventure quite thrilling enough without complicating it at this stage.

One thing you may immediately expect is a radical transformation of your outlook on life, for you will have changed forever the relationship of your mind and your physical body. No longer will you regard your mind as being limited to your body: you will realize that you are in essence something much more, something that is capable of independent survival. At the same time, you will be aware of your responsibility toward your physical body and will feel a loving regard for it, for it is your home, and your vehicle of expression, during this present incarnation.

You will need to assimilate these matters, and you should on this first occasion return to your body after passive contemplation of the astral scene in which you find yourself.

## Substance and cord

On subsequent occasions, when you begin your exploration of the astral world, you may find that in order to travel any significant distance you need to send back astral substance to the emotional and instinctual region of your psyche. This is achieved by an act of will, a brief determination to return excess astral substance to the astral body.

Once you have the *feel* of astral projection, you will, as was pointed out in Chapter 1, "travel light." In other words, you will instinctively learn to regulate the amount of astral substance you send forth for general purposes of astral journeying. There will still be occasions when you need to send back more of this substance to the body—in traveling through time, for instance, or in ascending to higher and more spiritual levels of the astral world.

You will see clearly the astral cord that connects you to your physical body when you have projected; but when you travel away from your body the cord will become attenuated and may disappear. This does not mean that this vital link between your body of light and your physical body has ceased to exist, however. The link cannot be broken or dissolved, and even if you can't see it, it will still be operative.

## Returning to the physical body

When you are in your body of light upon the astral plane, you should not approach too closely to your physical body unless you intend to re-enter it, for you might be automatically drawn back into the confines of your material being. Such an occurrence is termed "snap-back," and is quite common in unconscious astral projection.

When you have completed your astral excursion and you wish to return to your physical body, proceed as follows.

## *The Return*

1. In your astral body, repose yourself about eight feet above your physical body and facing the same direction.

2. Now "will yourself" to descend slowly into your physical body. *The levels of your psyche will automatically re-engage when you do this, and you will return to wakefulness in the material world.*

3. Complete the operation by performing the Foundation technique, so as to ensure optimum coordination of levels and proper distribution of all psychic energies.

### *And just in case . . .*

If you used the third method of astral projection given here, *The Going Forth*, and you created an astral figure into which to transfer your consciousness, but you went to sleep before completing that transfer, then you should reabsorb the astral figure when you awake.

In such a case, proceed as follows:

# *Reabsorption Following Sleep*

1. Return the figure to the state of a luminous silver-gray cloud and re-absorb it through the cord.

2. Reabsorb the cord.

3. Finally, conclude with the *Foundation technique.*

If you used the first, second or fourth methods of astral projection but fell asleep before achieving success in transference of consciousness to the astral dimension, then, when you awake:

Perform the *Foundation technique* to realign the levels and to adjust the psychic energies.

This is important, and you should where necessary pay particular regard to this tidying procedure so as to maintain control of your energies and to ensure proper enforcement of the rules for the benefit of the astral level of your psyche.

# 9

# Astral Travelers,
# Astral Folk

---

*Unintended projection • Earth-level contacts and
exchanges • Listen and learn: but rely on your
own judgment • A problem in astral communication
• Spiritual teachers • Review the teachings you receive
• Elementals • The question of remanence
• Astral imprints • Character of the elementals
• Your role as leader • Friendship with elementals*

---

From time to time you'll assuredly meet with other astral
travelers. A number of them will take no notice of you,
being literally wrapped up in their own concerns. They may
not even be aware of their surroundings. Projection can take
place in various circumstances, and frequently without intention or even consciousness of it. You can only leave those
people alone, as might be the case in earthly life if you saw
folks drifting along looking blank, or talking to themselves.

On the astral, such people may not be talking entirely to
themselves. It sometimes happens that someone intent on
planning an important business conversation, for instance,

through deep concentration passes without noticing it into a mild trance—they would not notice a loud crash, or someone speaking their name—and this can easily pass into a projection of consciousness into the astral. Often someone while lying in bed at night will work out an important conversation for the next day, and doze off into trance while thinking about it.

Subsequently, one of two things can happen. Either, to the planner's astonishment, the other party will—for better or worse—speak exactly the words that were imaginatively assigned to him or her; or else, mysteriously warned of a far-from-obvious drift, he or she will venture into no part of the leading topic.

Then there are other types of unintended astral projection. There is the occasional nude, of either sex, and most often adolescent, who suddenly comes to a halt, stares around at the scene, then down at his or her own form, utters a yell, and vanishes. Don't worry, that person just awoke from a rather strange dream! People soon learn to clothe their astral form.

## Beginners and others at earth level

Astral drifters of any type, however, are only likely to be encountered fairly near to earth level. As you become more expert, you'll meet fewer of them. Even though for various reasons you may wish to move close to earth level yourself, there will be a difference in "vibration," and your practiced attention will be focused more exactly upon what you seek.

You may love Earth's scenery and desire to climb the Andes in safety, or to walk the jungle unarmed and yet uneaten, or to glide through the ocean's depths in perfect freedom. Or you may in fact be a keen explorer in the flesh, but desire a preview of some untried cavern or mysteriously deserted territory.

## On the astral road

At earth level or in any other astral region you visit, you are likely to meet with kindred spirits here and there. You can exchange views, impressions, and ideas with them just as with chance-met travelers on earth. Listen to them and learn. Every person's experience can be an asset to you, as yours can be to them. But don't be over-impressed. Always, as on earth, use your own powers of judgment and decision.

Although all your perceptions will be beautifully clear, you may find at first that your astral thinking is slowed a little. This is because you don't have quick access to all the facts that are stored in your physical brain. Practice will enable you to carry over more data, but it's as well to remember that other astral travelers can have the same problem, and may be speaking with less knowledge and wisdom than they suppose.

Do people speak in the astral world? Do they walk? The answer might seem to be yes in both cases, except there's no language barrier in speaking, and you can walk where there's nothing to walk on. The truth is, many things are done differently in the astral world, but until you are quite at home there you'll find it easiest and quickest to act as if you were in your physical body.

## Spiritual teachers: all kinds

On the astral, as on earth, the differences in outlook and experience between individuals is limitless, and the exchange of ideas on an equal footing can be of great value to the participants. The teacher-pupil relationship, however, is another matter. It needs careful handling, particularly if you are the pupil.

For many people it's a secret dream, to get away out of their body to some high plane, to meet and receive guidance from the teacher, the sage, the guru, the master of their aspirations. Such things can happen, and the effects of an experience of this kind in the life of the recipient are apt to be lasting.

There are many reasons, however, why an experience that seems to be of that type may not be the genuine article. You may not be moving on a particularly high plane. For every genuine teacher, sage, guru, or master who is to be met with in the nonmaterial worlds, there are a host of beings, human and other, who wish to be such.

Not all seekers for power and admiration are dreadful sinister fig-ures. Many are all too human and sincere and, when one understands them, rather pathetic figures, but they can tell you nothing you should lay to heart permanently.

And not every genuine spiritual teacher and guide ought to be your personal teacher and guide.

How, then, can you tell what you should heed?

Until you are fully at home on the astral, and can command all your faculties there as fully as when you are in your body, there's only one safe course of action.

## Do your thinking at home!

Enjoy the delight of being taught, of having your mind and imagina-tion directed to new viewpoints. Promise nothing, make no inner commitment or undertaking: a true teacher does not want a rushed as-sent. In any case, try to impress upon your memory every part of what you are told or shown.

Then later, when you are back again in your body, take the first op-portunity to sit or lie down quietly, recall and reflect upon what you learned.

There are several reasons why you should do this.

If you decide you were given good counsel, which was *right* for you with your outlook on life and at your stage of earthly and spiritual progress, you'll need to familiarize your whole self—including your brain-power—with the teaching.

Alternatively, you may on reflection decide the counseling was not wise, or was not suited to you at this time for one reason or another.

## Careful here!

Certainly you ought to reject even the most seemingly sound advice if on consideration you feel it's all wrong for you; that you just couldn't live with it. But spiritual teaching that is right for you will generally hold one drop of wholesome bitters in the sweetness. It will call you to rise a little higher than you wanted to go just yet. That may be the very reason why you needed to hear it.

By contrast with this, teachers on the astral who simply wish to attract a follower are usually skilled enough readers of a person's emotional state to know what you'd find pleasant to hear, to catch you on a weak spot.

An example of this kind of bogus spiritual leadership would be to tell someone who is studying for a tough degree that they ought to give it up now and renounce all earthly ambition. Don't fall for that kind of thing! It may perhaps be your destiny to become a hermit on a small island, but get your degree first and then review the situation.

## Sunlight is an antiseptic

This is another good reason why you should take time to review your astrally received spiritual teachings. By bringing each item into consciousness, you can decide whether you want to adopt it or dismiss it; and if the latter, you can dismiss it effectively, knowing your reasons, without some forgotten clause becoming a subliminal and acting as an unrecognized factor in your motivations at some future time of decision.

Using subliminals is like planting a garden: the results can be wonderful, if you get what you want from a reputable supplier. You need to know what you are burying in your garden.

That's another good reason for learning to project voluntarily and in full consciousness.

Almost everyone makes an excursion into the astral world at some time or other, consciously or not. Almost anyone may pick up ideas, sentiments, or impulses without knowing where they come from or whose mind formulated them. If you travel consciously and with purpose, you can afterward sift your collectibles, remember the character you had them from, bring them out into the sunlight, and decide which ones you want to keep. When you are an advanced astral traveler there will be no need to postpone this review until your return.

In the realm of ideas, sunlight and the conscious reason have much in common, and a great antiseptic quality.

## People of the astral world

Then there are the elementals, native inhabitants of the astral world.

Some travelers don't meet with them or notice them. Others have a great affinity with them, and often have already made their acquaintance by means of etheric sight, without leaving the body. For them, a main incentive to astral projection is frequently the chance to follow up that acquaintanceship to greater advantage.

The elementals inhabit a region of the astral world very close to earth level and containing many of the same features, but influenced more strongly by the more subtle of earthly conditions. It does not go along quite consistently with earth time, however. Frequently one meets with the condition the dowsers call *remanence*, of which the observer might quote:

> *That which has been is now, and that which is to be has already been* . . . .
>
> Ecclesiastes 3:15

This state of things helps to make this region, which is a sort of borderland between earth and the astral, a most interesting and often surprising place. The elementals themselves manifest in all shapes and sizes, generally with some relationship to the element (Fire, Air, Water, or Earth) and the life-style they are most accustomed to. A person with etheric sight may have been puzzled by the persistence with which amphibian-type or even fish-type-appearing entities, obvious water-lovers, will cling to a dried-out river-bed and disport themselves in it as their natural right-of-way. But when that person projects consciousness into the true elemental world, the dried-out-gulch is revealed in the full glory of a foaming torrent and the delight of the elementals becomes understandable.

Again: in renovating an old mansion, a ruined part of the building may have been torn down, with the result that a branch of the stairway now runs up into the blank face of a new wall. So far as the human residents of the house are concerned there is nothing more, and some odd sounds heard occasionally from beyond the wall remain inexplicable. But astrally, the demolished part of the old mansion can still be there, and is very likely inhabited—not, as the residents of the refurbished part may imagine, by human spirits, but by elementals playing one of their favorite games as make-believe humans.

## Elementals as impersonators

Sometimes a human resident of past time may have left a strong emotional imprint at a low astral level, expressive of physical pain, short temper, or so on. Of course these imprints could, by themselves, be discerned by a sensitive human percipient, but it's also possible for an elemental to discern them, and to take on the role of the person in question. In the case of a child or adolescent, no strong emotion need be involved, for elementals generally find a stronger affinity with young people than with mature adults.

Elementals are usually gentle beings: not through any moral principle—for they have none—but because any entity that might be hostile to them is most often on a different waveband. They have a great capacity for fun, with a tendency to practical jokes, and if they gain access to a superabundance of energy from any source they can go boisterously wild. In their natural way of living, however, their innocence and playfulness have a refreshing charm that tends to fascinate the beholder, while their strange beauty seems to be drawn from all the kingdoms of nature.

## Elementals as friends

If you are the sort of person who can have animal friends, most likely you will innately understand what is needed in friendship with an elemental.

There are differences. Because many elementals are more or less human in appearance, and because in an earthly relationship you don't generally get the impression of an animal speaking to you in words, you'll tend to talk with elementals with more confidence of being understood. In reality, unless an elemental has already had considerable experience in relating to humans, the way you look, move, and sound are more important than your words. The elemental may perhaps pick up your meaning telepathically with more accuracy than the animal. We can only judge by the response.

There is another difference, an important one. When once an intelligent animal is past the baby stage, it will carefully maintain certain preserves of time, for activity as well as for sleep, in which you do not share. You on your side are also understood to have your own occupations. With an elemental it is entirely you who must set those boundaries, and you must set them firmly. You must remain the leader and thinker.

Still, there should be recognized playtimes when you relax and allow yourself to be led, allow yourself to be shown the wonders—and the fun—of the elemental world. You'll realize how much care is taken by your elemental friend, or friends, to discover what will most delight you.

What can you give in return? Abundant, and sincere, manifestations of pleasure and thanks. Further, you should take care always to make it clear that although relatively little of your time can be given to this friendship, it holds a very special—a unique—place in your regard.

These delicate beings who live entirely at the astral level—the level of the emotions and instincts—if they enter into friendship with a human, become as hungry for that person's approval as small children, and develop the possessive jealousy of cats. To win the abundant joy of such a friendship, you will need to have patience, understanding and, at all times, strength.

# 10

# Friends and Helpers

---

*Astral encounters • Meetings with discarnate human spirits • Resources for knowledge and understanding • Apparitions and the etherically perceptive • Astral shells • Appearances at the moment of death • Spiritual friends and helpers*

---

If you are deeply interested in astral projection, whether or not you have yet mastered the art of performing it of your own volition, you may very well encounter, in various ways, others who dwell or travel in the astral world.

A pair of friends or lovers—people already known to each other in their physical existences—can enjoy astral travel, fun, and adventure together. If initially only one of them can achieve astral projection at will, that one can help and teach the other.

## If you are an astral traveler

In the course of your astral travels you may strike up a friendship with another astral traveler. This has great possibilities. You may meet with a kindred spirit who, in the unlikely event of your meeting on earth, would be separated from you by a language barrier or a generation gap. Or you may meet someone who's sat in the same office with you for years, and neither of you would have dared speak of such a subject as out-of-the-body experience.

You may have a fascinating encounter with a real adept of time-travel. You may possibly meet with extraterrestrials. Or you may make friends among the elementals, and return again to some corner of the astral universe where you know a delighted welcome awaits you.

## Meeting with the discarnate

You don't, usually, just casually meet up with discarnate humans on the astral—that is, people whose earthly bodies have died. Those you do meet are likely to be wrapped up in their own musings or quests, or in some degree of shock after an unexpected ejection from bodily life, as after a sudden accident; or, for similar reasons, they can be quite unaware as yet of their bodiless state. (They will, after all, have the astral body; and you'll know by your own experience how solid and adequate a body of astral substance can be in the astral world.) Mostly these people will go their own way, but occasionally one may appeal to you for help or advice.

If that happens, it's best not to reply with any kind of dogma or philosophy. Take the situation as presented—that is, after all, that person's perception of it—be gentle, and avoid shock. Go on your own knowledge of astral conditions, and answer accordingly.

For example, it's not unheard of for some discarnate one to complain that since their recent sickness their nearest and dearest will not speak to them, behaving as if they weren't there.

You may meet with bewilderment or disbelief, or a more painful reaction of grief or fear, if you try to make this person realize the loss of the physical body. Leave that discovery to come slowly and naturally. The person is, after all, very literally in an altered state of consciousness, and most likely experiencing a traumatic level of dissociation. You can however give the questioning soul some practical and helpful advice: to go and talk to the loved ones while they are asleep. You can convey confident hope as to the outcome. That way you'll not only help the person out of an emotional cul-de-sac, you open the way to reassurance in dreams for the bereaved family, and you put the puzzled wanderer in a position to learn from them the circumstances he or she needs to know.

While it is not generally a good thing for a discarnate person to remain earthbound for long, still a clear understanding and acceptance of the situation makes onward progress easier than it is for someone who remains preoccupied with a need to find out what happened.

## How to help and advise

Circumstances can differ widely. Nobody knows everything, but if you draw without prejudice and without haste on all the resources available to you, you probably can arrive at more knowledge and understanding than you are aware of.

In your astral being, you are in touch with all the levels of existence. You may not be consciously in communication with your Higher Self, but you can and should seek enlightenment from it at any time. You have the conscious and instinctual resources of your astral being, and you can summon brain knowledge from your physical body to guide you, as well as bring over reserves of energy for whatever you may wish to do. The technique of bringing over knowledge or energy is only gained by resolution and practice, but that's the way to increase your competence in astral living. You simply "will" what you need to come to you, and then wait, patiently but resolutely, until it blossoms in your astral awareness.

## If you are not a traveler

Astral friendships and meetings of the kinds suggested above can, likewise, come within the experience of the etherically perceptive person who is not, at least volitionally, an astral traveler. (Although whether one is in the body or out of it who can say, when entranced by the beauty of some lonely forest or waterfall, one becomes aware of the elemental dwellers in the place, or when out of one's sleeping dreams one responds to the cry for guidance of some baffled soul?)

There are some happenings, however, which seem more particularly to befall people who are in their physical bodies, regardless of whether they are able to project their consciousness astrally or not. The sight of apparitions is such a phenomenon; and with it must be included the equally common, though less often mentioned, experience of astral sounds or odors.

These things, naturally, seem less strange to the astral traveler who, if she or he experiences them at all, will clearly perceive the elemental or other being that seems ghostly if partially seen in an earthly setting. Similarly, astral sounds and odors fail to seem strange if one is in the astral world and can see their cause and origin.

Nevertheless there is also a low region of the astral world that is filled with phantasms and astral debris of all kinds. An astral traveler leaving the body is most likely to bypass that level unless for some special reason she or he makes an effort to enter it. For a person in the physical body, however, the case is different. The faculties of psychic perception vary, not only from individual to individual but also for one person from time to time. A person needs only to be slightly more perceptive than average, and/or the density of an astral phenomenon needs only to be slightly greater than average, and the person becomes aware—or partially aware—of it.

## Astral shells

The apparitions known as "astral shells" do not qualify as either friends or helpers, nor is there anything you can do for them, or that they need. Still, they are fairly often seen, and an understanding of their nature is a good starting point.

What, then, is an "astral shell"?

The lowest level of the psyche, as we've seen, enmeshes with the physical body. The only function of that part of the psyche—the "gross astral"—is, precisely, to integrate psyche and physical body. In astral projection the gross astral, or most of it, remains in the physical body, keeping it alive and well while the consciousness is elsewhere. At the complete separation of the psyche from the physical body at death, therefore, the gross astral has no longer any purpose and is discarded.

Several things are possible at that point. Usually the gross astral remains with the physical body and rapidly disintegrates. Sometimes however—and quite often in cases of violent death from whatever cause—the gross astral, not having become naturally outworn or exhausted, may become separated from both the departing soul and the physical body, and continue existing for quite some time before it ultimately disintegrates. In the meantime it drifts around, as completely lifeless as a photograph, keeping either the customary appearance of the deceased, "in his habit as he lived" as Shakespeare puts it, or representing with startling vividness the appearance and manner of that person's death. Both fact and legend are full of stories of such apparitions. They can be disturbing or even shocking, but are completely inert and harmless and, of course, are not in any way suffering.

## "Moment of death" apparitions

Also related to this separation of the gross astral, but quite different in character, are the fairly frequent instances of someone at the moment of death appearing to a dear friend or relative, maybe just to give greeting, maybe to impart some special message, but not manifesting again. The dying person has the will to make that visit, and on quitting the body does so: the availability of gross astral substance, no longer retained by the body to keep it in life, gives the consciousness of the released psyche a vehicle dense enough to be perceived by a person with, perhaps, not very acute etheric awareness.

After that momentary occurrence the gross astral is most often discarded in the normal way, and no further appearances occur.

# A different type of apparition

Certainly not all psychic appearances are accounted for in the ways described above; and here we come to our spiritual friends and helpers.

Sometimes it happens at a critical point in one's life—perhaps at that time it is an unsuspected critical point—an incorporeal visitor gives a word of counsel, of warning, of hope or reassurance, as may be needed.

This visitor may be a friend or relative who quitted earthly life quite a number of years before. It may be a kindred spirit whose creative works or other achievements you've deeply admired, although that person may have left incarnation before you were born. It may even be someone of whose identity you have no idea, or a being of non-human—perhaps angelic—nature. Instances of all these have been known. The visitor may speak to you with or without audible voice, when you are awake or, more likely, when you are asleep.

# How do you know?

The first point you, or others, are likely to question is that of your visitor's identity. Is it who it seems to be, or another entity, or a part of your own unconscious mind? (Or, for that matter, part of someone else's unconscious mind—not impossible within a family group!)

Here let it be confessed: you will generally have nothing to guide you but your own deep sense of the visitor's identity. The only confirmatory evidence you can have is if the visitor gives some sign or clue whose significance you only discover later; and even this is not conclusive. Your inner conviction of recognizing an individual character, a personality, remains the only standard you have to go by.

# Different levels of dream

Here a word of caution—and encouragement. If such a visitation comes to you in sleep, and your recollection of it on waking is mixed with dream stuff, obvious fantasy, don't *simply on that account* decide it must be spurious.

If while you were dreaming, a flesh-and-blood person were partially to rouse you from sleep and say something to you, quite possibly on recalling the incident you might find the speaker's words had woven themselves into your dream so as to make it hard for you to be sure what really happened.

Your dreaming mind has many levels, which can be occupied with different ideas and imagery. When we remember a period of dreaming we automatically try to rationalize the dream so as to make one story of it, but, even so, it occasionally defeats us. Then if we were telling of our dream, we might have to say something like, "I dreamed we were having a party at home, and yet at the same time I was in a boat on the river"—or some such thing. In the same way, your disembodied visitor may not have the power to engage every level of your sleeping mind, and yet may have something very real to tell you.

## More important than "Who?"

However overwhelming may be your sense of the identity of your visitor, or however painfully you may wish it to be some certain person, this is not, however, the most important consideration regarding messages of this sort.

It's true that people and other beings in the nonmaterial worlds can sometimes get a longer overview of what's brewing on the astral than we have on earth. It is equally true that by no means everything that appears on the astral will come to fruition, or need come to fruition, on earth. Furthermore, people who made mistakes in their earthly lives—and that's most people—are not going to become pillars of wisdom by the simple act of dying.

This does not mean that you should discount such messages. On the contrary you should give them, not authority in your life, but very careful thought. Always remember this: whether a message comes from an angel in heaven, from your grandfather's grandmother or from your own unconscious, nothing can alter your invariable responsibility, to decide consciously on the course of your own actions.

# The astral helpers

To turn to an entirely different form of communication during sleep:

This happens sometimes to people who can, and do, project into out-of-the-body consciousness of their own volition. It also happens to people who can't, including some who never desired or believed in such a possibility.

All these people have, however, some special aptitude, known or un-known, some special skill that can help others (or that can help *one other* in the universe). At one time or another, these people are taken to exercise that skill, that aptitude.

Sleeping, they have been raised up, not into physical wakefulness but into astral consciousness. They have found two luminous beings awaiting them: most often two, and unknown, but inspiring unques-tioning confidence. These two, like expert swimmers conducting a novice, have taken the sleeper swiftly through astral ways to do what-ever is required.

# Your special task

If you are thus guided, you may find the person you are to help is someone you know, directly or by hearsay. Or you may not know that person at all. You may have to encourage that person to live, to die, or to be born. You may have to calm a grief, soothe a terror, dispel a nightmare, dissuade a would-be suicide, help fight an addiction, any one of innumerable things. The person you help may be incarnate, or may not.

Whatever it is that is needed, you—you in particular—can do it, because of who you are, because of what you know, or because of some mysterious bond between you and that other.

To people who have had such an experience, no matter how skepti-cal they may be in general, the full reality of that episode is something they do not doubt; nor does the sense of reality fade as a vivid dream would fade with the passing of time.

# 11

# Exploring the Cosmos

---

*Journeying at astral level in the material universe
• Ideas at large in the astral world • Riding the
current of popular interest • Exploring the unknown
• Past or future insights? • Brain-knowledge and
the deeper levels of the psyche • The cosmic bridge
• Points of reference • Astral exploration of space*

---

Let's imagine you now have the "when" and "where" of your astral travels under control.

You have passed through the early novelty stage of making astral visits to friends. Probably you've found that to avoid startling them and to contact them easily for a good exchange of ideas, it's best to make your visit when you can be sure they will be physically asleep. A person's sleeping mind doesn't have the "these-things-don't-happen" barrier that is ingrained into the waking consciousness by bad early training.

You may be able, from that point, to get your friend to travel astrally with you—a topic we shall return to later. But, whether in company or alone, you may very well at some time decide to travel out from earth, to venture into the illimitable wonders of the cosmos.

This is not a venture into higher spiritual realms. To travel spiritually higher is certainly to find, at some point, a level beyond which one cannot rise because it is the limit of one's present spiritual attainment. That is, nonetheless, always a worthy and exhilarating endeavor. What is meant now is journeying at astral level in the material universe, the selfsame cosmos of planets and stars, meteors, nebulae, and the rest that astronomers study through their telescopes.

Since mere distance is no obstacle to astral travel, you can, theoretically, get to any point in the cosmos.

In reality, however, there is another factor involved, a rather curious one which will enable you to travel astrally, at a given time, to some places more easily than to others. This factor applies to some extent with regard even to earthly localities, but is much more noticeable and powerful in cosmic travel.

Although its effects are considerable, this factor is generally unremarked and there is no familiar term or metaphor for it, so let's call it "the trodden path factor."

## The "trodden path" factor

If you have not already experienced it in some form, you assuredly will do so as soon as you begin to use your initiative in psychic matters.

With regard to cosmic travel on the astral plane, it works like this:

Supposing, of your own volition and for reasons entirely personal to yourself, you develop a strong wish to pay an astral visit to Saturn's moon Titan. You look at charts of the heavens, you picture the long marvelous flight to Saturn and thus to Titan, but the venture fails to gain reality: you can't somehow get a grip on it. Once an idea is turned loose into the astral world it is fairly sure to be picked up by some hungry seeker for inspiration; and so your wistful mental images of Saturn get picked up by a writer with little concern for scientific likelihood, but a great talent for capturing the popular fancy. Suddenly the newsstands are filled with a fantastic tale about a captive heroine on Titan, held prisoner on a rock in the midst of a lake of methane.

People read the story and ask, "Where is Titan?" Many of those people in their turn will look at charts of the heavens, will picture the long marvelous flight. Now you try again, and behold!—the astral doors are open. You may have to struggle through a phantasmal array of swordsmen and monsters, but you can do it—you can get through to the real Titan, moon of Saturn, with the unbroken stillness of its rocky landscape and its veritable lakes of methane.

## There are always pioneers

Likewise, if there is a sudden great turning of interest to some more distant part of the heavens—to Sirius perhaps, or to the jewel Betelgeuse—if you so desire, you can ride that current and go where otherwise maybe you could not.

*Or maybe, in any case, you could.* To be a pioneer in anything is tough, it's true: yet there are always pioneers. So if you feel there's still an unknown dark planet in our solar system awaiting your discovery, or if the Pleiades call to you, or Aldebaran, or if you yearn to taste at closer range the mighty zodiacal influences—who is to set a boundary to the powers of the psyche?

So much, then, as to your possible choice of destinations. As to the journeying, the gliding onward through the deep vistas of majestic beauty, the sudden nearby burst of prismatic or white-fire refulgence, the color-changes of suns and skies through atmosphere and space and perhaps an alien atmosphere again: this is often the most unforgettable part of cosmic travel. Maybe you could cover the distance in the twinkling of an eye—but you are not likely to choose to.

When you arrive at your destination, however, what will you find?

## Time-slip

Supposing you visit a planet—say Mars—which, over vast periods of time, passes through a series of climatic phases.

Usually your main perception will be of the present condition of the planet. There can be variations to this, however, and particularly so if the present phase is a quiescent one.

Just as a sensitive person walking in a great modern city can suddenly be overwhelmed with the almost living reality of the quiet villages or the wild scenery of past times, so it can be for the astral traveler on a strange planet. Further, the traveler on a strange planet has generally little or no historical knowledge regarding that planet, and is certainly not likely to have any knowledge that is ingrained enough to be helpful at the time of the experience. Afterward, back home and in the body, the traveler may reflect that some of the things seen must have related to a past or future phase of the planet's climatic cycle; but that will call for reference to the brain's stored information, if not for a consultation of reference books.

## The bridge of books

It is a fact that if you want to follow out a quest in the cosmos, there are two things you must do without fail. One is to spend all the time you can, each night, looking at actual light from "out there." The other: you must read all you can lay hands on concerning the celestial object of your inquiry.

This reading is of immense value in several ways. To begin with, you can't have too much brain-knowledge of any subject that interests you. Then if your interest is enthusiastic (as in this case it ought to be), the more attention you give to this brain-knowledge the more of it will penetrate to those deeper levels of your psyche, to be readily available to your consciousness when out of the body. But that is not all. By reading you are, both consciously and unconsciously, contacting the minds of the people who wrote those books, people who have also been enthusiastically interested in the subject.

For the student and the practitioner of astral travel, to read with deep attention of any region of the universe—of any time present, past, or future—is in actual truth to make from the words, and from the writer's thought and imagination behind the words, a *cosmic bridge* (to borrow a phrase from August Derleth) *into another time and place.* The real and potent magick of books is in the contact of minds they provide.

## The broader the base, the higher the tower

Nor should your reading be too narrowly confined to the exact topic that fascinates you at the time. Like a gem, your favorite topic will show to better advantage in an appropriate setting; and your grasp of the subject will be of greater value to you if you bring to it numerous points of reference or comparison.

Besides reading, collect pictures—illustrated books, astronomical pictures from magazines, science-fiction pictures if they appeal to your sense of space. You'll not only want close-ups of planets or stars, your imagination will also enjoy pictures of deep starry vistas in which to anticipate your journeying.

Your collection may well include, too, views of starry skies above ancient monuments of earth: the Acropolis at Athens, the Egyptian or American pyramids, Stonehenge, or any great shrine or similar place where through long ages human minds have continually lifted from the earthly scene to the illimitable heights beyond, and have taken wing in irresistible aspiration.

All cosmic pictures will become bridge-builders for you, and here you are likely to observe a curious sign of promise. Even if you tell nobody about your collection of cosmic pictures, you'll find more of such pictures begin coming to you. This, indeed, will hold true whatever the subject of your collection if it is a matter of real enthusiasm to you. Before you yourself are drawn forth to the real goal of your seeking, tokens of it will be drawn, in a seemingly unexplained way, to you.

## Cosmic travel

Your area of interest being defined, and thoroughly pursued, by reading, by looking at pictures, and by astronomical observation, the astral technique involved in your intended travel will be as follows:

## *Astral Exploration of Space*

1. Commence with the *Setting apart of the place*.

2. Lying down, perform the *Foundation technique*, and then proceed to enter the astral world by projection.

3. In the astral world, bring to mind all that you can concerning the object of your quest, and let your emotional response to these things encompass you, let it bathe you and inspire you. Fleeting astral images may present themselves to you at this point, relating to your thoughts.

4. Now rise high above your astral location, into the astral equivalent of the upper atmosphere and beyond, to the edge of space.

5. As you rise, if necessary send back by an act of will some of your astral substance, so that your ascent is swift and unimpeded.

6. Halt your ascent.

7. Consider the world below you; look at the pulsing currents of the living aura of the planet; and look outward, into the deeps of space, at the jeweled and vibrant splendors of the cosmos, and at the particular region of your interest.

8. Your position in relation to the cosmic scheme of things being thus affirmed, formulate clearly the intention of traveling to the place or phenomenon of your quest.

9. And now speed forth to your adventure.

# 12

# Times and Places

Just as taking a walk is good physical exercise, and involves a greater number of muscles than you might suppose, so also your astral journeying will bring into play many more of your psychic faculties than you need give a name to.

All of these things are very good for you as a whole person.

## Reaching into the past

Suppose, now, that instead of going out into space in your astral travels, you decide to go to a particular point in earth's past history.

You may know of the experience of someone who has done such a thing involuntarily. Perhaps the someone was you. In any case you want to know now how you can have, voluntarily, the experience of traveling astrally back to a past time: either where you are now, or in some other region of earth.

## The vital link

If you can examine the facts of a few such experiences, more often than not you can find a link between the person and the time and place they visited. Certainly the link is always there, although it may not always be apparent.

It may be hidden in the ancestral or incarnational background of the person who had the experience.

For that reason, it is not always possible to follow exactly in the steps of a person whose astral explorations you may wish to emulate. Unless that person and yourself are in some way close enough psychically to be able to travel together, your best course is to look for the times and places for which you personally feel the greatest affinity. You do not need to know consciously the cause of the affinity. Probably in time it will become clear to you; but it will work for you before then.

## Factors within your control

In choosing goals for astral time-and-place travel, however, there are many factors within your control. Often a person who has an astral experience of going back into past time has simply heard or read or looked at something—music, a book, types of clothing, pictures of historic buildings—or more powerfully still, has handled an artifact from the time and place in question. Then, whether immediately afterward or later, off they go to visit the time and place with which the psychic link has been made.

So you, too, want something, a sample, a witness, to link you with the time and place you desire to visit astrally.

An artifact, or the sound of appropriate music if we are thinking of historical time, or a fossil if we are going back to the earlier ages, are among the strongest possible links: something you can handle or hear, experience, or live with.

A powerfully produced movie can be very effective, even if it isn't totally accurate. When the time comes, you'll find yourself making the necessary adjustments.

Pictures come next as a connecting link and, where a special place or region is involved, a map can be surprisingly effective. Gazing at the map and approaching your objective upon it from as nearly as possible your physical direction (that is, from the west if you are west of the real place, from the southeast if you are southeast of it) you should be able to follow the map's various features toward your objective, then look at that point on the map and say to yourself "I want to be *there*."

This doesn't mean that when you travel there astrally you will follow in conscious laborious detail every road, railroad, river, or mountain range that leads you that way on the map. Apart from any other consideration, you'll travel too rapidly for that, but going over the details in imagination first certainly helps ensure the outcome.

## When a material link is needed

If your desire is to visit a past time in some distant place with which you do not have, so far as you know, any personal bond, then you ought to have a really strong link, preferably a material object, to ensure success. If you are in the United States now and you want to visit eighteenth-century Turkey, or Siberia in the time of the mammoths, and you have no personal connection with whichever place it is, then you ought to have a piece of eighteenth-century Turkish tile, or a Siberian fossil—even a piece of fossilized moss—of the period in question, as the case may be.

## Capturing an adventure

When you are holding the object, remain silent, and first notice the way it feels so you will remember this. It may feel cold or warm, light in weight, or heavy. Where there is much psychic influence objects often seem surprisingly heavy for their size and material. It may even seem to give out a kind of tingling sensation that is not altogether physical.

Just occasionally you may have the experience of feeling you don't want to proceed further with a particular object. If that happens, you should take heed of it and stop. Fortunately such happenings are uncommon, and you can expect a warm feeling of increasing reciprocity with the object and its associations.

After establishing contact with the feel of the object, you should briefly imagine yourself deliberately drawing in its influence, willing yourself to do so. Then for the rest of the time stop trying to do or think of anything. Just passively receive what the object has to say to you.

Then turn your thought to the appropriate time and region. Imagine your witness taking its rightful place in the scene: your tile in its position upon a wonderful tiled building, dazzling with color in bright sunshine, or your moss as fragrant, living moss growing in a wide, peaceful landscape, in the pleasant, temperate climate Siberia once had.

## And without a material "witness" . . .

But you may not by any means be in a position to touch, even for two minutes, any material object relating to a particular period in history that fascinates you.

No matter! "Where there's a will there's a way"—a proverb whose truth has been proved many times over; with regard to astral matters it is plain fact.

### Use what comes to hand

If your will is set on traveling astrally back to the Rome of the Caesars, you can condition yourself powerfully to do so before you embark on your out-of-the-body experience, even if you have nothing more to help you than a photograph of a coin of the period and a map of central Italy. (Note that in such a case it's a good idea to have the map *and* some other form of witness, such as the pictured coin.)

Even if you have no more than the map and a picture of a bust of a Roman character who interests you, you have enough; even if you have no resources but to gaze at Rome on the map and repeat to yourself the name of Livia Augusta or Mark Antony or whoever else is the focal point of your interest and curiosity: still you have enough.

This is not an excuse for slipshod preparation, but if you are resolute you will not be slipshod. Make the best use of whatever you can find that will link you with the place and the time you desire to visit; but when you are making that best use, be assured it is enough.

## Psychic barriers

By using these simple methods of preparation you will be enabled, when you go out on to the astral, to visit almost any place and time of recorded history you may desire—from judging for yourself of the beauty and magnificence of Cleopatra, to seeing what life was really like for your own great-grandparents. Some great riddles of the past, however, you may or may not be able to solve by going and looking.

What exactly was said and done at the Mithraic initiations? Or in the Mysteries of Eleusis? Some astral travelers see those things; they have a right (incarnational, evolutionary, karmic, whatever) and a need that draws them to inquire into matters of that kind; and so they go back in time and gain the knowledge of them. Because they are aware that the right and the need are something especially their own, most often they say nothing about it.

You, yourself, may be such a person, with or without conscious knowledge. Or, of course, you may not. Intense curiosity about a hidden matter is no guarantee of deep-level involvement, although it is a pointer worth following up.

If you try astrally to look into something that is effectively protected against trespassers, and if in fact you are a trespasser—well then, you will not succeed in that attempt—that's all. There is no punishment, for there's nothing to punish. The trespasser simply does not get through that particular hedge. At least, not at this time. Psychic and spiritual life is progressive, and the trespasser may not always remain a trespasser.

## Astral time travel program

Taking these factors into account, then, our journey into the astral past can be accomplished by the following method:

## *Astral Past-time Sequence*

1. Commence with the *Setting apart of the place.*

2. Be seated comfortably. If you have suitable, evocative music, play it softly during these preliminaries. Remember, you will be using this music to create atmosphere and to send signals to the emotional-instinctual level of your psyche, so you will not want it to be intrusive or to engage the attention of your rational faculties.

3. Consider your witness, make contact with its *feeling*. Then will yourself to absorb its influence.

4. Remain seated, passively experiencing whatever comes to you from the witness, allowing impressions to rise into your consciousness.

5. Turn your thoughts to the period of history that interests you, and see your witness taking its rightful place, playing its part, therein.

6. If you are using a map, consider the route you will follow. Look at the destination point and say, "I want to be there."

7. Lying down, perform the *Foundation technique*, and then proceed into astral projection.

8. When you enter the astral light, bring to mind the atmosphere of your witness: then make a mental resolution to go to the specific place and time of your quest.

9. Now speed forth upon your journey, following the route you previously decided upon. *As you travel you will find that you progressively*

*return through the years, increasingly so as you near your destination. The scenes through which you pass will reflect this regression, changing about you as you proceed.*

## Discovering your powers

As you gain facility in this technique of astral time travel, you may—after performing the *Foundation technique* and before proceeding into actual projection—formulate a specific intention of finding yourself already in the desired period of history when you enter the astral light; and upon entering the astral light you will make your resolution to travel to a specific place in this period.

In such an event, the astral environment in which you first find yourself will be completely different: you will not see your physical body, and your surroundings will be those of your location *as it was* in the period of history you are going to explore.

It is also possible to project from the outset—seemingly instantaneously, although very swift astral travel will actually be involved—to both the time and the place of your quest. Again, the formulation of specific intent, following the *Foundation technique* and before projection of consciousness into the astral world, will be necessary.

But these refinements of technique are skills for you to discover as you gain experience. Ultimately their successful use will depend upon:

- The efficacy of your preliminary work: of your true contact with the feeling of your witness and the absorption of its influence by the deeper levels of your psyche.

- Your real understanding and constant use of the powers of your astral body.

## The return to the present

Return from the astral past presents no difficulty. When you have completed your exploration, you simply *will* yourself to return to your physical body in present time. You will immediately travel to it, passing through the advancing years and, depending upon the speed of your flight, the changing scenes. When you reach your body, you re-enter it by the usual method, and upon returning to everyday consciousness you conclude with the *Foundation technique.*

## Astral travel into the future

The past is fixed, and you can travel back into the real past as it was. The future is still mutable, and when you go forward into it you can only travel into one of the possible futures, one of the ways it can work out.

Is, then, any foretelling of the future nonsense?

Not at all! But you need to know how to understand and use it. The same is true of the future into which we can travel astrally.

Since no preview of the future is irrevocably fixed, your prevision gives you the advantage of taking a hand in its shaping. If you like what you foresee, you can work both materially and psychically to bring it about. If you dislike it you can, equally, work to prevent or to modify it. And whether you accept it or wish to change it, you can— except in instances where other people may be working to produce a contrary result—be quite sure of success.

## Coping with panic situations

Even when there seems to be a strong current of opinion going against yours, there are occasions when you should still resist that current astrally: not only because for the public good you ought, but also because, if your standpoint is positive and the opposing standpoint negative, you have a very good chance of turning the tide.

Examples of this occur when, as a result of some ill-advised utterance, there is a strong public current of unreasoning fear or hate. Such an emotion, reflecting from earth level to the astral, can easily be reflected down from the astral to earth again and can thus seem to have gained a higher authority.

Many good and sane people, struggling against such a current at earth level when it is already fully developed, may find they are not strong enough to quell it; but if you and certain others (who may not be known to you) can fight the thing in the astral world, foreseeing it before it is fully developed, you can succeed. It is like diverting a stream in its small, shallow upper reaches, instead of trying to battle with the raging torrent it will become in its lower course.

## Bonus for astral travelers

This ability to take direct action in the astral world is a real advantage that the astral traveler has over the clairvoyant. What a talented clairvoyant perceives may certainly equal the perceptions of the astral traveler; but the clairvoyant, being able to act on those perceptions only at earth level, is subject to all the delays and contentions that attend earthly existence.

Here is the kind of happening that illustrates this point and at the same time shows up clearly the changeable nature of future events. This type of occurrence is on record, but instead of merely citing one example, the sequence of events can best be given here in general terms.

A clairvoyant of recognized powers and integrity foresees a disaster involving catastrophic loss of life. The prevision is usually clear and explicit, including place and time, the names of some of the dead and injured, and the technical cause of the occurrence. On returning to earthly awareness, the clairvoyant resolves to reach the authorities involved, with a view to preventing the calamity.

The first negative reaction of officialdom against taking notice of a psychic warning does not need to be described. Only the known character and abilities of the seer leads someone to take a look at the facts. The names of the predicted victims are indeed those of people who will be at the given place at the time in question, so finally an inspection is made and the technical defect discovered. The calamity, with its resulting deaths and injuries, is effectively diverted.

# If . . .

The uncertainties and hassles of the whole thing, worked out at earth level, are obvious. The astral image of the calamity was evidently complete in every detail, just ready to come into material reality. If the clairvoyant had been less known and respected, if any one of the officials had been more obstinate and had refused any action that day— or if the names or the technical details given by the clairvoyant had been incomplete—then the warning might have failed to prevent the disaster.

An astral traveler can deal differently with such a situation. On seeing the cause of the problem in the Astral World itself, the traveler can create the astral image of its being found and resolved before the time of imminent danger; then, to make assurance doubly sure, the traveler can probably move into the ambience of earth and, still astrally, visit a sleeping technician and impress on him the need to check all details at the earliest opportunity.

## True prediction, changeful event

The incident outlined here makes its second point very clearly.

With time and place, names of persons and the nature of a genuine technical defect all correctly given, with the fact that disaster would inevitably have followed if this had not been dealt with, nobody could doubt the reality, the truth of the prediction. Yet, in plain fact, the foreseen calamity *did not occur.*

In such a case, what is the truth of the matter?

What the clairvoyant in the above example saw—and the kind of thing you may at some time happen upon if you explore the future astrally—is a possible, even highly probable, future development of an existing situation. But given right and timely action at astral or even at earthly level, disaster can be avoided.

The fulfillment of no prophecy—absolutely none—is certain and unavoidable.

If you want to utter predictions, prophecies, based on your clairvoyance or your astral travels—and if you want to be certain of telling the truth—then prefix every statement you make about it with "This I saw," or "This I experienced." The fact that you saw or experienced it remains true, even if you yourself see good cause to do everything possible to avert its coming to pass.

## The bright side

Why so much gloom, however?

Undeniably, people with a flair for looking into the future, by whatever means, seem to come back with tales of impending woe more often than not. They have done so through the ages, though people generally, in spite of it all, enjoy life rather than otherwise. The astral world as a whole, too, is a place of wonderful joy and beauty.

Perhaps there ought to be a strict limit to the time we spend in deliberately looking into the future, even for the purpose of averting clouds of threatening harm. Perhaps the greater part of our time in the astral should be spent in helping create the future: contemplating its blissful realms of innocence, from the elemental region up to the abode of those shining ones we call angels—they, too, are of the astral world. From those places of light and joy, let us send back and bring back vital impulses of light and joy to earth. Many people will pick them up, knowingly or unknowingly; they will act and speak with gladder, kindlier hearts as a consequence, and the world can only be the better for it.

# 13

# Astral Love and Sex

*Love in the astral world • Astral sex—different from*
*earthly sex • Love, passion, and play in earthly sex*
*• Orgasm in astral sex • Astral sex and earthly*
*happiness • Elementals • Astral-to-physical sex*
*• Astral and earthly codes • Twin psychism*
*• Love, death, and the astral*

L ove is a word that has meaning at every level of being. At
each level this meaning is somewhat different, even
though there is enough of a shared basis of significance to
justify using the same word.

However, love in the astral world is love very much as
most humans understand it: strongly emotional with much
influence from the instinctual and physical side of life, but
also with incursions and illuminations from the mental and
spiritual levels.

The word "sex" has a few meanings, too; and the fact that
several of these meanings are often to be found confused together, is—well, that's the nature of sex.

About astral love, then, there's no problem; but clearly, astral sex is not the same thing as earthly sex. Certainly it can

feel the same—it can feel like earthly sex, raised to a high mathematical "power"—but it can't be the same, because the bodies involved are of astral substance, not of earthly substance. Nor can our thoughts about astral sex be contained within the conventional framework, because human law and custom alike are geared to regulate the conduct of earthly bodies, not of psychic entities.

Such a variety of questions are always raised by the topic of astral sex. It seems best to consider a number of them now as question and answer, insofar as answers can be given.

## Love, passion, and play in astral sex

- *Question:* Can people on the astral plane, out of their physical bodies, really feel sexually attracted to each other?

  *Answer:* Certainly they can, and it often happens, because sexual attraction is both emotional and instinctual, qualities that belong essentially to the astral level of the psyche of sentient beings.

- *Question:* Can that attraction find expression and fulfillment in astral union?

  *Answer:* Very definitely, and without the limitations bodily structure places upon even the most enthusiastic earthly lovemaking. The partners can, temporarily, merge their bodies of astral substance in a total union if they so desire.

- *Question:* Might an astral union of that kind be a pledge of pure love?

  *Answer:* It can be a pledge of the deepest and purest love, just as earthly union can, if that's what the partners intend. Or—also like earthly union—it can express and slake the burning astral desire that underlies physical passion. It can also express the lighthearted generous intimacy of happy playfellows.

  It can be any and all of the things earthly union can be, but it can convey them far more completely, because body language as known on earth is inevitably less flexible and less expressive than astral body language.

- *Question:* While a pair of lovers embrace on the earth plane, is it possible their astral bodies meanwhile go into the kind of total union you've mentioned?

  *Answer:* There's nothing to prevent that, and it could be the reason why their physical bodies are sometimes irresistibly drawn to merge likewise.

## Orgasm in astral sex

- *Question:* Can a pair, making love while out of their bodies, experience real orgasm?

  *Answer:* They most truly can: repeatedly if they wish, or for one long sustained period such as is practically unknown in earthly experience.

- *Question:* Surely that must be exhausting?

  *Answer:* On the contrary. Such orgasms do spark off a lot of energy, and a little of it is lost; but mostly it's exchanged between the partners, and the rapid exchange of charges of energy is exhilarating. It's one of the delights of astral sex.

- *Question:* Surely it would be fun, then, for two who were lovers on earth to go out on the astral together for the special purpose of making love that way?

  *Answer:* Surely, and in fact a lot of couples do that. But, also, it's fun for a lot of people who don't know each other on earth at all.

- *Question:* Do you mean that during my astral travels I might meet an attractive person who was also out of the body, and we might wander into some astral nook and enjoy a wonderful rapture, yet never know each other in the flesh?

*Answer:* That would not be unusual, and it might remain simply a brief astral romance. But, due to the nature of the astral world, such lovers quite often do meet together in their earthly lives at a later time, sometimes brought together by the most unlikely circumstances.

## Astral sex and earthly happiness

- *Question:* After such a wonderful astral experience, surely an earthly relationship might be disappointing?

  *Answer:* Perhaps; but earthly relationships have their special sweetness, too, even in their very imperfection. If the two partners could go out on the astral together any time for a special thrill, there would be no loss. They would have the best of both worlds.

- *Question:* In my earthly life I'm not a great success with the opposite sex. I lack the finer points of physical attractiveness. Given that my astral being is perfect and radiant, as stated, does that mean I can look to the astral world for romance and happiness?

  *Answer:* Initially that's a great objective. But you should and can hope it will not be the whole story. When you discover your powers of attraction in your astral life, you'll progressively strengthen and enhance your astral body in that respect, and build your self-confidence too.

  What is brought to pass on the astral plane can come to pass on earth. In a while you'll begin to walk tall in your earthly life, too, knowing yourself to be a vibrantly attractive person. Then your earthly life also will fill with interest, with romance and happiness.

- *Question:* My partner and I love to bring fantasy into our love life. Sometimes we pretend to be two characters out of a movie that interests us. Sometimes we pretend to be two strangers who have just met. Sometimes we just swap a few clothes and pretend to be each other. Can we do things like that in astral projection, change our real astral shapes one way and another?—or would that be too weird?

*Answer:* Nothing's too weird for the astral world. Imagine different scenes and watch them come into existence around you, change your own forms too. Be, and do, what you please. Variety is of the essence here: this keeps anything from becoming too real. Astral fantasies are enjoyable while they last, and, too, the memory of them gives an added sparkle afterward to everyday life—and to every night life also!

• *Question:* I've had several love affairs, but each one ended because I became sure it wasn't what I was looking for. The missing factor is not sentiment, or affection: I need a sense of physical fulfillment I don't get, and yet I get all there is to have. Is astral sex the answer for me?

*Answer:* You may at some time have had some subliminal astral adventures—that is, not conscious enough to remember, but not unconscious enough to forget. To go back consciously to find similar experiences may well be the answer for you. At any event, the astral view of things may very well make clear to you what it is you're seeking. If it's something outside the range of your present life circumstances, then for this lifetime keep it astral. That way you can be content without making anyone else unhappy.

## Those elementals

• *Question:* What about elemental lovers? They seem so fascinating.

*Answer:* The give-and-take of energies, which to humans is such a thrilling part of astral sex, is an exhilarating pastime for elementals, too, but not in quite the same way. Many elementals delight in being humanlike, and to be loved by a human is the ideal of those. But they don't have the same scale of values that most humans have. What in earthly life we should call lighthearted flirtation is, to an elemental, a very normal aspect of friendship. But if they attempt the deeper levels of love, they tend to develop an unreasonably jealous possessiveness. So keep it light!

There's another reason to do so. The boundary between the elemental level of the Astral World and this world is thin and delicate, and a repeated giving of your energy and probably astral substance to an elemental could cause the breakdown of that boundary, to the disorganization (to put it mildly) of your earthly life. This is no mere theorizing: such strange and embarrassing things have happened to unwary humans.

- *Question:* I take it there's safety in numbers as the old proverb puts it? I've had some experiences of group sex on the astral, and somehow there has generally been an elemental or so involved.

*Answer:* Yes, even when they don't participate, elementals love an astral orgy. The atmosphere of wild excitement naturally attracts them, and they can enjoy a lot of flying energy. They may join in, either "as themselves" or for the fun of being taken for humans, and sometimes it seems they set the scene for the occasion.

## Astral-to-physical sex

- *Question:* What about sex between two partners, one of whom remains in the physical body? I can do astral projection, my partner can't. Soon I shall be going on a long business trip. Doubtless I can make an astral visit, but can we have sex?

*Answer:* Sure you can! And it's a special experience. This is one of those instances where you'll do well to let your partner know beforehand, in a general way, your intention of visiting. Someone who goes to sleep in a pleasant, hopeful mood will be attuned at all levels for your visit; however, any considerable degree of anticipatory arousal could easily close the doors of true astral awareness, and perhaps prevent sleep.

But you shouldn't miss the opportunity. In the astral exchange of the embrace itself, the astral partner is likely to gain more gross-astral substance from the embodied partner than is usually available to the astral traveler. That is true, even though some gross-astral substance, more than is needed in ordinary astral travel, is spontaneously brought over from the physical body for sexual activity. When one of the partners remains in the physical body, therefore, the astral partner can be so amply provided with gross-astral substance as to be near materialization, and the experience is memorable for both partners. It is the all-encompassing ecstasy of astral sex, together with the real and intimate sensations of near-physical intercourse.

- *Question:* If the male partner is the one who is out of the body in this type of intercourse, surely if he has an orgasm he'll be snatched back into his physical body?

*Answer:* There are two reasons why this doesn't necessarily follow.

One is simple: this astral traveler is, in the nature of the case, at a considerable distance from his physical body. Unless his physical body is threatened by any danger, the possibility of his being involuntarily snatched back, as you put it, is minimized.

The other reason is more significant in the present context, and needs to be understood. Don't mistake the nature of orgasm! It is not the same as ejaculation. If it were, orgasm would be impossible to women. It is a spasmodic high of sexual feeling, belonging physically to the autonomic nerves and, psychically, to the astral body. The glandular response to the nerves is secondary, and many men learn to control it consciously. Certainly until he has some practice a man may tend to snap back into his physical body at this point, but if in his ordinary sex-life he has practiced nonejaculatory orgasm (which has several advantages besides this one), success with it in astral intercourse will more easily be his.

- *Question:* Could I have astral-to-physical sex with someone I don't know in earthly life?

  *Answer:* If the other person is ready and willing, there's no problem. It could be a happy surprise for both of you. But those are the necessary conditions. If the other person were not willing, you'd probably not succeed, plus you'd give the other party a nightmare, plus you might cause that person to be laughed at or suspected of delusions.

- *Question:* Can a child be conceived through astral-to-physical sex?

  *Answer:* We can't give a definite "yes" or "no." Law and common experience say "no." Tradition and a knowledge of strange happenings say "could be." Certainly there are instances where a child has a startling resemblance in looks and temperament to an impossible parent. Sometimes direct astral-to-physical sex seems to be the operative factor, but in other instances a more complex procedure seems indicated. The curious and constant factor is that in every likely example of whatever sort, a definite intention to produce the child can be stated of at least one parent.

- *Question:* If I travel astrally to visit my lover who has no out-of-the-body experience, can we both go out to make love on the astral plane?

*Answer:* You might mean two things here.

Your question may be simply, can you help your lover get out of the body. Yes, you can. A method is given later in this book by which an astral traveler can help any companion out of the body, whether a lover or otherwise.

Alternatively, you might be asking if the altered state of consciousness which is induced in quite a number of people by orgasm, be strong enough to lift a person into astral consciousness. It could; and, where enough free astral substance is surrounding the couple, true out-of-the body consciousness could result, but evidence suggests that the attention centering on the physical plane causes this astral consciousness to be of very short duration.

## Astral and earthly codes

- *Question:* How can the limitations placed on earthly sexual relations be disregarded in considering astral relations? About a year back during an out-of-the-body trip, I encountered someone who was psychically very much my sort of person and who, in spontaneous astral projection, was seeking a lover. We've since met astrally a number of times, and our relationship has become an important and precious part of my life.

    Now, in the curious way such coincidences happen, without any seeing I've discovered beyond any possible doubt the earthly identity of my dearest one. And this is someone I could not for a moment think of having such a relationship with in earthly circumstances. Yet I can't break the astral relationship. What am I to do?

*Answer:* Do nothing. You give no hint as to what precisely the difficulty is about your lover, but as Carl G. Jung points out, the psychic reality of a person can differ in a number of possible ways from their earthly terms of reference. From what you say, your lover either has no idea of the problem or isn't worried about it. It can be considered, then, as entirely your problem.

Quite naturally, you don't know yourself well enough to see at once what is, for you, the right solution. Therefore wait and see. The problem will doubtless work itself out in one of two ways.

Your discovery may in fact matter to you at a deeper level than you now suppose, really making the relationship untenable. In that case, that fact will of itself work through into your astral relationship, gradually changing your attitude to your partner (and your partner's attitude to you). At last, inevitably, it will cause a break-up, but without hurting either of you as much as you now imagine.

Or that may not happen. Perhaps, after the initial shock of your discovery has faded, you'll cease to trouble about earthly circumstances, which cannot touch you or your lover as long as you keep your relationship entirely to the astral world. In that case, the two of you can go on delighting in that relationship for whatever time may prove to be its destined course.

## Twin psychism

- *Question:* I am one of a pair of identical twins, but in fact our close resemblance is physical only, and in other ways my twin and I are very different persons.

  A couple years back I taught myself astral projection, chiefly to be able to escape to somewhere I could stop being a twin for a while. At first this worked really well, but then I discovered astral sex.

  It's embarrassing. Although I've kept all my other astral activities entirely secret, everything I do that's concerned with astral sex gets back into my twin's dreams. Naturally this is causing a lot of curiosity and joking.

Why is my twin getting this feedback? And how can I stop it?

*Answer:* The probable reason for what your twin is picking up is that your adventures in astral sex involve more of the gross-astral level of your psyche than your other astral activities do. Your twin, whose resemblance to you is, you say, mainly physical, may therefore when sleeping pick up the denser levels of your astral activities more easily than the finer ones.

Be that as it may, telepathic communication between twins is a very real and well-recognized phenomenon. You can't just disconnect it. You can, however, divert your twin's attention to something more interesting.

The effective way to deal with a problem is very often the opposite from what we feel like doing. That is what makes it a problem. So why not change your attitude—it hasn't worked out very well anyway—and teach your twin to perform astral projection? Then the two of you can leave the body together. But, since you evidently differ from each other in mental and emotional make-up, once on the astral you'll part company and each seek out your own experiences.

You may even find that it's fun to compare notes afterward.

## Love, death and the astral

- *Question:* When our earthly lives are over, can my partner and I hope to remain as lovers forever in the Astral World?

  *Answer:* If you and your partner love each other truly and lastingly, then for a certainty much higher levels of the psyche than the astral one are involved for both of you. That gives a much better prospect for the kind of reply you want.

  This may seem like a paradox but it isn't. In itself, the Astral World gives no stability to anything within it. Although we may revisit a person or a place in the Astral World many

times, it is our own will or another's that gives the necessary
stability to the astral situation.

You and your partner, too, like everyone else, will assuredly
evolve and develop. But, given that the higher faculties of both
of you are in charge of the situation, there's a tremendous
amount of most interesting and valuable activity on the astral
that a loving duo can take part in for an age not measurable in
earthly time.

This ideal view of things can certainly be fulfilled. But
if you want to reinforce your optimism with a rather lower-
pitched reassurance, then at least be certain of this: despite the
changefulness of everything in the Astral World of which we
can be conscious in the ordinary way of etheric consciousness,
there is a more hidden level at which nothing that is, or that
has been, ever completely passes away. Like the rings in a tree
trunk, however they may be compressed by later growth, every
detail of the history (of the tree, of the person or of the world)
goes on existing and making its contribution to the whole.

Besides, on account of your present life and love, you and
your partner are both without any doubt different people in
some important particulars from what either of you would
have been if you'd never met. This also remains true, whatever
may change, and has its place in molding the destiny of you
both.

# 14

# Astral Healing

*The astral world: the level at which healing begins*
*• The gift of energy • Informing another of*
*intended help • An astral visit • Astral sight: looking*
*beneath the surface • Working on astral substance*
*• The discolored clouds of infection*
*The astral matrix • The pure radiance formula*
*• Looking with knowledge and understanding*

All healing begins on the astral plane. Strictly, it begins higher than that, but the astral is the level at which we can get to it and help. Two reasons; *one*, the astral is the world in which the great powers of spiritual being and mind-life can meet, and through the medium of the astral can en-mesh with the heavier and slower potencies of physical being. And—*two*—the emotional and instinctual life of the sufferer, which needs to take a major part in the process, is itself in and of the astral world.

The astral is the level at which we can *help* the healing process. This is said not merely as a matter of modesty, and not simply to guide the practical psychic to remain within the law: for in truth nobody, not even the most highly qualified member of the medical profession, can do more than help the healing process that, if it is to take place at all, must take place within the material and nonmaterial levels of the total being of the sufferer.

## Taking and giving

To put our helping in the broadest possible terms, it can be considered under two heads: the *removal* of something the sufferer would be better off without, and the *giving* of something the sufferer needs.

The latter requirement is most generally recognized as the province of the psychic helper, for there is one gift, energy, which needs little skill to give, and which is very welcome to a person afflicted with anything from a fractured limb to chronic depression.

Further, a sufferer with sufficient reserves of energy can frequently cope with the other part of the program if that is needed—getting rid of whatever would impede healing—without too much difficulty.

However, in that area, too, there is often much that can be done by the psychic helper, particularly by one who can act on the astral level.

## Telling the recipient

A person for whose well-being you mean to do any astral work should always be told beforehand of your intended help. Not necessarily, unless you know they can take it, that you are going to leave your body in order to give that help, but that at a specific time you will be with them in spirit, or in mind, as they may understand it. People often use such phrases, forgetting the words were originally meant to have a quite literal meaning; this may give you a chance to lead your friend gradually to a realization that the truth is better than they had hoped.

At all events, something should be said as to your intent. That is not only good ethical practice (and good manners); it gives the person the cheer and encouragement of your purposed help, and also means he or she can be more cooperative with your actions on the occasion itself.

This is not at all contradicted by the fact that you'll try to choose a time for your astral work when the recipient will be asleep. It is the physical body that sleeps: the psyche, the entire nonmaterial part of the person, will be awake, every level in its own manner.

For this reason, there would seem no grounds to limit the obligation to tell your intention of astral work to those who are in fit condition to indicate that they hear you. The comatose and the delirious, for instance, may very well be aware of what you say to them; the student of states of projection should, of all people, have no problem regarding this.

## If someone refuses?

As a matter of fact there is no problem if you are thinking simply of the positive side of the matter—that of giving the recipient a chance to cooperate in what you will be doing for them. Even if you don't get through to the person's conscious mind you may get through to some level of their unconscious, their Deep Mind, and this can be even more important and effective. If, finally, you don't succeed in getting through at all, you have lost nothing by trying.

There are instances however—rare ones, certainly—where a conscious person will refuse psychic help of any kind. There are people who feel it would in some way be against their faith; there are the less logical ones who will have nothing to do with it in order to prove they don't believe in the possibility of it; and there are certain ones who fear that a lessening of their present woes will doom them to greater ones.

In these cases or any others you may, of course, seek gently to reason with the person if you feel able to do so: but it should remain clear that the will of the sufferer is the ultimate deciding factor.

"But a delirious or unconscious person," someone may point out, "can't say 'no' even if they want to." That is very true. Most often they don't want to. Sometimes it seems the person's conscious mind has been temporarily put out of action, precisely so the great instinctual forces of life could have a free hand in the healing. But in a few very rare cases, even an unconscious person may refuse help, and may just clam up inwardly when you make your astral approach. They may have deep reasons.

You can't do more than fulfill your obligations in these matters.

## An astral visit

Supposing, then, the preliminaries having been settled, you go astrally to visit a sick friend. For a purpose of healing—and, indeed, for many other purposes—the visit is best made at night. For one thing, when a person is asleep, or at least drowsy, the emotional-instinctual nature is dominant, and since this itself belongs to the astral world your task will be easier on account of it. For another thing—and this is another important consideration—there is less danger, particularly after midnight, of the sick person being disturbed by *embodied* lookers-in.

As an astral visitor, you will at first glance see your friend just as you would if you were present in the flesh. One difference: if the room is in darkness, you will see clearly although probably without losing the sense of it being nighttime. Then, however, in order to help whatever is amiss, you may need to see literally what goes on beneath the surface.

## The importance of looking

Most likely you'll know beforehand where the trouble is. That makes your task easier, but in astral work a great deal is done by means of looking.

You should not underrate this part of the proceedings. Even if you know for a fact that your friend has a torn ligament, a fractured bone, a ruptured (or simply troublesome) appendix—or whatever—you still want to see, astrally, so you can fix your attention upon it.

## Seeing what's inside

In this matter, as in others, astral sight is a matter of attention. Here's a parallel from daily experience and physical seeing, because in this, too, attention is important.

If you want to see if a window is clean, you look at the glass; and even if something quite strange should be happening out beyond the window, you might not at that moment notice it. If on the other hand you look through the window for the purpose of seeing something on the other side, then you pay no heed to specks or smears on the glass and they may not even come into your visual focus.

So, from force of habit, naturally your first astral look is at the outside of your friend, as if you were in your earthly body. Then, astrally, you can if you wish look "through the window" of a person's exterior. You can see into a person's internal organs or cavities, bone structure, or muscles—even into the circulatory and lymphatic systems, should this be required.

When you have found the seat of the trouble, you can work on it.

## What you really do

It will seem to you exactly as if you were working on your friend's bodily structure: the physical nerves, muscles, heart, stomach, or so on. In reality you are working on the astral substance that underlies, enmeshes with, and maintains the bodily parts in question. This knowledge ought not to puzzle you or hinder you in your actions: it simply explains why those actions are effective.

For instance: supposing this is a case of a fractured bone, fragmented at the point of injury. With your astral hands you can bring the fragments together, replacing and reshaping the parts of the bone as they should be; then from those hands you bring astral substance, you charge it by an act of will with energy for healing, and with it you cement the repair you've just made, packing and covering the fracture with it.

Then you can return to the exterior of your friend, smooth and soothe the site of the injury, and bid the sleeper to sleep soundly and awake refreshed and recovered.

It may in most cases take a little while for the physical body to catch up with the astral pattern, but your help will have been to great purpose. There is, as you may be aware, another level of the astral body—one further removed from the earth level—at which the injury has not existed at all; and that is the pattern to which the healing physical body will try to conform, and will conform all the more closely because of your help.

It will probably be obvious to you, as a matter of reason, that you have not mended a physical bone with astral substance, although that is what you saw your astral hands doing. The substance on which you worked was your friend's astral substance that was enmeshed with the injured bone. You restored that astral to its proper form, you added astral substance, energy, and well wishing of your own—all of which should hasten the swift, natural, and healthy healing of the injury.

## How do I cope with infections?

You can see an infection astrally; in fact, if you have well-developed etheric sight, you can see it even while you are in your physical body.

Because it is not a part of the sufferer's own astral being, the infection generally appears as a discolored cloud or patch of mist covering the affected part of the body. In the case of a virus or other infection that affects the entire person, when you have the knack of looking at the right astral level for these signs you will see it as a discolored mist overlying more or less the whole figure, though even so there may be a focal point of especially intense discoloration in one physical area, depending on the nature of the trouble.

The colors of these infection clouds are always murky and unpleasant—a bluish or yellowish mud color, a red or green clouded with brown or gray—because by their poisons they throw the right functioning of the sufferer's energies into confusion.

If you have a particular interest in these matters and gain some experience in them you will soon get to know which colors denote, to you, the presence of a particular malady; but on subjects of this kind one psychic observer will not always agree with another, valuable though each one's observations may be for personal use.

Curiously enough, when there is a bad psychic influence (as when one person, perhaps unknowingly, depresses another, or upsets another's nerves), the same kind of discolored cloud appears over the face or perhaps the solar plexus of the sufferer; again, it is not a part of the sufferer's own psychic make-up.

Whatever the cause, you need a technique to deal with these clouds.

## Working on the astral matrix

This is an instance in which you (whether in your body or out of it, but more directly and powerfully if out of it) can work upon the astral manifestation of a condition and change it, so that the effects of the change will in turn produce change on the material level.

There is in fact a very real relationship between the adverse emotional conditions and the bodily infections that manifest so similarly at astral level. Neither microbes nor viruses *necessarily* infect, and the hit-and-miss immunization given by our daily contacts is not the whole explanation. Someone who might ordinarily travel unharmed in a bus full of sneezing people (who all ought to have stayed home anyway) is likely to fall victim to their colds at once if he or she has lately sustained some emotional shock or stress.

With regard to accidents, too, Freud was certainly right in paying great attention to the possible factors of consent and of unconscious self-inducement; while Jung's concept of synchronicity and our own knowledge of psychokinesis place the possibilities in that line at a far higher level. What we *will*, unconsciously in particular, may be quite different from what we consciously desire. That is one reason why it is so important in this work that the sufferer should formulate, and should if possible utter, a positive wish for wholeness.

These discolored astral clouds, therefore, which you discern at the site of the bodily or psychic malady, represent something very real that needs to be dealt with at the nonmaterial level. (There is of course no reason whatever why the sufferer should not receive help at the material level also; we are not concerned to prove the power of faith, or the power of psychic action; the only objective that matters in this is the restoration of the person concerned to health and well-being, at every level and by whatever means are available.)

We can, then, regard these astral clouds as a phenomenon in themselves, which can be treated directly. There are several ways in which they can be either dispersed or transformed. The following is recommended because it is effective without needing high psychic development on the part of the operator.

## Bringing a reality into focus

- Your procedure here is to focus certain realities in your mind's eye and make them as vivid as possible to yourself.

- You realize them in relation to each other.

- Then you institute a certain movement.

- If you insist on seeing things in a certain way in your imagination you can mold the substance of the Astral World accordingly.

    *This is your own creative faculty at work.*

- This change in the Astral World then brings about a change in the material condition that corresponds to it.

    *That is the "causal" property of the astral light at work.*

- Everything you are doing here is thus in accord with known psychic and occult laws.

## *The Pure Radiance Formula—Method 1*
### *For use while in-the-body*

1. Perform the *Foundation Technique*.

2. Spend some time in contemplation of the work you intend to undertake.

3. Look at the person you are going to help. Consider the appearance and location of the cloud formation(s) indicating the infection.

4. Next, imagine high above you a sphere of intensely brilliant white-hot light. Recognize this light as completely present and potent in the work you are doing.

   If you can simply accept the reality this represents—and it is a reality—fine. But if you need to relate that white-hot radiance to an idea, you can think of it as "the Spiritual Sun" or "the Divine Light."

   *Don't in any way let what you are going to do here be directed back to your personal self.*

5. Having fixed this high point of the Spiritual Sun or of the Divine Light in your consciousness (perhaps feeling a flash of sheer joy in your mind because of its effulgent beauty) turn your attention back to the person you are helping.

   Fix your gaze on the discolored astral light: if there is more than one region, concentrate upon the largest area, the main location of the trouble. Intensify your astral faculties to see it as clearly as possible.

   Then, by a deliberate act of your will, make it revolve in an counterclockwise direction.

   Remember, you are manipulating the image so as to gain control of the reality.

   Keep the Spiritual Sun formulation, or the Divine Light formulation, in your consciousness as you do this.

6. Make the discolored patch of light turn faster. See how, as it does so, it becomes larger and more diffuse, less related to the sufferer.

7. Then, with the same whirling movement, see the discolored light becoming detached, fragmentarily at first, until the whole of it goes flying up into the burning whiteness of the Divine Light.

   Some particles glow for an instant, then all has vanished in the whiteness. The discolored light is consumed, absorbed in that brilliance. It is cleansed, and transformed back into pure energy, freed from all taint and dispersed afar through the universe.

8. Look back to the person you are helping. The area of discolored light should have vanished. If there were smaller regions of discoloration, chances are that these were caught up in the rising vortex and have gone also.

    If any part of them, or a vestige of the main area, should remain, you can do a general mopping up operation with another counter-clockwise vortex, whirling, diffusing, and sending all the fragments flying up to transformation and dispersion in the Spiritual Sun.

9. Now seal your work with light, as follows.

    Look to where you have set the brightness of the Divine Light, the Spiritual Sun. Drawing a deep breath, therewith pull a beam of its radiance into yourself, deep into your heart like a blessing.

    Let it remain thus for a moment.

    Then, bringing its luminous power out along your arms and through your hands, hold your hands close to the location of the trouble (the region where you saw the main discolored patch of light), and pour that mighty power into it. See light and power slowly spread from the location of the trouble, until the whole figure lying before you is aglow with it and vibrant with energy.

10. Now mentally pronounce this blessing:

    *Be every function and part of this person, in body and*
    *psyche, infused and vitalized with Divine Light, so that*
    *all may be brought into the harmony of right measure*
    *and balance without lack or excess.*

11. Conclude with the *Foundation technique*.

## Sharing the experience

For a serious or widespread infection, or for deep-seated depression, you may need to repeat this procedure on successive occasions. As far as you can, let the person you are helping understand the various stages of what you do; if talk during the session would be distracting, choose some other time for the telling. Immediately after a session, however, the best thing the person can usually do is sleep.

Whenever and however you explain your procedure, its power for good will be greatly enhanced if the sufferer can envision the various acts with positive acceptance along with you. This beautiful and joyful procedure is, besides, a great lifter of spirits.

If two heads are more effective than one, two hearts are immeasurably more so!

## When a sleeper awakes!

As given above, the *Pure radiance formula* is intended to be used by a practitioner who is *in the body.* As such, it is certainly of great value, and can be instrumental in assisting a sufferer's recovery. It is given in that form for use by students of astral projection who may have a need to employ it, but who are not yet proficient in the technique of willed projection of consciousness onto the astral plane.

Used in connection with the technique of astral projection, however, the *Pure radiance formula* is greatly augmented in power; and because it is thus made real, the practitioner can be more confident of providing successful astral treatment for a sufferer's condition.

When carrying out the procedure astrally, it's best that the person you are visiting should be physically asleep throughout your activities. That will not hinder—and it will probably make easier—your getting through to your person and communicating at the astral level.

Once a real rapport has been established, however, so that bewilderment and shock are avoided, this rapport and the continuity of your actions can remain unbroken even if your person wakes up in the course of the session.

Should this happen, wait quietly in your astral presence. If your person is aware of you and speaks to you, just answer astrally. When the person settles again, sleeping or merely relaxing, you can resume your intended procedure.

There are minor sequential differences between these two methods of the *Pure radiance formula;* but the major difference will be found in the intensity and richness of the astral experience itself.

# *The Pure Radiance Formula—Method 2*

## *For use while out-of-the-body*

1. Using your preferred method of astral projection, enter into the astral light.

2. Having come astrally into the presence of the person you are going to help, spend some time in contemplation of the work you intend to undertake.

3. Look at the person who is the subject of your work. Consider the appearance and location of the cloud formation(s) indicating infection.

4. Now, by an act of will, bring into being high above you a brilliant sphere of light. Realize this light as being completely present and potent in your work. It is a symbol of the Spiritual Sun, or the Divine Light.

   *The substance of the Astral World will respond to your*
   *thoughts, and the light will come into manifestation*
   *above you. Its degree of presence will however depend*
   *entirely on the strength of your creativity; so spend some*
   *time in formulating the light and meditating upon it,*
   *so as to bring it to vibrant reality.*

5. Having fixed this light in your consciousness, and being astrally bathed in its radiance, turn your attention back to the person you are helping.

   Fix your gaze on the discolored astral light: if there is more than one region, concentrate upon the largest area, the main location of the trouble. Then, by a deliberate act of your will, make it revolve in an counterclockwise direction.

   Keep the Spiritual Sun formulation, or the Divine Light formulation, in your consciousness as you do this.

6. Make the discolored patch of light turn faster. See how, as it does so, it becomes larger and more diffuse, less related to the sufferer.

7. Then, with the same whirling movement, see the discolored light becoming detached, fragmentarily at first, until the whole of it goes flying up into the burning whiteness of the Divine Light.

The discolored light is consumed, absorbed in that brilliance. It is cleansed, and transformed back into pure energy, freed from all taint and dispersed afar through the universe.

8. Look back to the person you are helping. The area of discolored light should have vanished. If there were smaller regions of discoloration, these should have gone also.

   If anything of them, or a vestige of the main area, should remain, you should initiate another counterclockwise vortex, whirling, diffusing, and sending all the fragments flying up to transformation and dispersion in the Spiritual Sun.

9. Now seal your work with light, as follows.

   > *Look to where you have set the brightness of the Divine*
   > *Light, the Spiritual Sun. Drawing a deep breath, there-*
   > *with pull a beam of its radiance into yourself, deep into*
   > *your heart like a blessing.*

   Let it remain thus for a moment.

   Then, bringing its luminous power out along your arms and through your hands, hold your hands close to the location of the trouble (the region where you saw the main discolored patch of light), and pour that mighty power into it. See light and power slowly spread from the location of the trouble, until the whole figure lying before you is aglow with it and vibrant with energy.

10. Now mentally pronounce this blessing:

    > *Be every function and part of this person, in body and*
    > *psyche, infused and vitalized with Divine Light, so that*
    > *all may be brought into the harmony of right measure*
    > *and balance without lack or excess.*

11. Now, by an act of will, cause the light of the sphere above you to increase so that you and the sufferer are bathed in its brilliance; and then see that light diminishing, and the sphere of light itself finally disappearing.

12. Return to your body.

# Knowing your subject

So far, it will be evident that any astral traveler, or even any person with developed etheric vision while in the body, can do a great deal for sufferers of many kinds.

If this kind of astral work really interests you, however, you should not rest content with what you can do.

Knowledge—brain-knowledge—does have real value if you are sufficiently concerned to get it down into the deeper levels of your psyche. This is done by making a habit of reading about various aspects of healing, reflecting on what you read, making it real to yourself, and relating the facts you thus gain to other facts you may have come across in your experience of life.

Don't keep any of your knowledge in sealed compartments. Reflect and relate continually. This will make everything you know so much more valuable, as the faceted gem is more precious, holds the light and sheds it more gloriously, than the uncut stone.

Certainly, in every instance you will *look*, etherically or astrally, at the person you wish to help. If you look with knowledge and understanding, you will better see what you are seeing.

Some knowledge of anatomy is almost indispensable. Then at least a theoretical knowledge of some of the manipulative skills can be a great help. Read books on osteopathy, reflexology, and the like, imagining yourself performing the various procedures described and, even more important, understanding as closely as you can the reason and purpose of everything.

You will not be working on the physical body, but the better you understand its needs the better you will know how to deal with its astral counterpart. Remember, you will *seem* in many cases to be working directly on the physical body; but in fact, reaching into the inner recesses without cutting or displacing anything, and making deficiencies good with a reinforcement of astral substance, you will be doing things that would not be possible on the physical level.

Add knowledge and understanding to your goodwill, and you will be able to help nature's healing processes most wonderfully.

# 15

# Your Astral Potential

---

*Examining in detail what is seen astrally*
*• Creations and adaptations • The astral root*
*• Charging a phenomenon with Light*
*• Astral employment of the Foundation technique*
*• The person of power*

---

To travel in the astral world is to find freedom in the world of ideas.

Certainly there are other techniques—scrying, meditation, directed dreaming—that can give clear sight into those astral regions that stand behind the material world. To enter the astral world in one's full consciousness gives, necessarily, the greatest opportunity for examining in detail what is seen. Besides, with practice other senses as well as sight can be used astrally to aid the observation; and other beings, human or elemental, who are met with, will often engage in conversation and will talk about the objects and occurrences which are familiar to them.

At first the astral traveler, or the seer, is so surprised and delighted with the wonders and the new aspects of the astral world that the relationships between these wonders and the phenomena of the material world are hardly noticed. However, there is no rigid boundary between these levels of being, and their interplay is continual. To our present purpose in particular, some objects or occurrences may be observed in the astral world that *certainly will* produce a manifestation in the material world, and many more may be observed that *easily can.*

Sometimes a degree of adaptation is needed, in substance or in mechanism, to suit the functioning of something astrally perceived to earthly conditions; but the astral traveler, or the seer, with the initiative and imagination to effect this, can have the pleasure—and maybe the profit too—of introducing an invention or a discovery whose success in this world can be easily assured. For the earthly version *already has* a firm link with an astral reality such as, in other circumstances, the innovator would need to build up with energy and perseverance.

## The work of human minds

Some of the astral objects and happenings most readily adaptable to earthly use are, not surprisingly, in the first place creations of human minds: whether the minds of such as have passed through the gates of death and are from one cause or another making a sojourn in the astral, or minds of powerful imagination—of artists or scientists who, probably without knowing it, are producing in dreams or reverie astral imprints that are coherent, explicit, and to some degree, lasting. Other readily adaptable phenomena are those of the realms of nature, which reveal, in a substance or a concept, characteristics which are constant at various levels of being.

For example: a person with the power of astral vision can perceive (even when in the body, but much more clearly and positively when the consciousness is in projection) the capacity of mineral substances, and crystalline substances in particular, to receive and hold impressions that can be scanned with delicate accuracy by the sensitive psychometrist or dowser; or which may affect many other people without their being aware of the forces involved. A conscious or unconscious perception of this kind may well have been the prelude to the invention of the quartz chip, whose imprinted message is accessible to anyone with the necessary technological equipment. In one sense, furthermore, the natural properties of the mineral inevitably *are* the prelude to the technological innovation, since, from level to level of being, the psychic matrix of the mineral varies only in its modes of expression.

## The "right" materials

When in projection, you should take particular heed of any phenomena that seem to belong uniquely to the astral world. The adaptation needed to reproduce the concept in earthly terms may be very simple, but also it may depend upon the existence and availability of the right earthly materials for its full effectiveness.

Garments worn by astral beings, for instance, do not as a rule have buttons or other fastenings, unless they reflect in detail some specific earthly style. Usually, whether clinging or loosely draped, they appear to be what they really are—an emanation from the person of the wearer—and they gain in dignity and gracefulness accordingly. A nineteenth-century princess came near to achieving this ideal effect with her ball dresses by having her maid sew the bodice seams upon her on every occasion, and unpick them afterward. This was considered extreme, even for a princess; but now with metal or nylon zippers we can all enjoy the same wholeness of line and freedom of movement, in everything from ball dresses to work clothes and parkas.

## Yours to observe

In marvels of light, color, and form, of sound, texture, and fragrance, the ever-changing astral world teems with continual manifestations of ideas, concepts, thought-forms and life-energies. All is yours to observe, to understand, to examine, and to inquire about; yours to reflect upon, while you consider analogies and lines of research.

But when you have found a concept or a type of energy that seems likely to reward your particular interest in its development, what if it changes and shifts, becomes something else, or is altered in its function and relevancy?

You can certainly continue your researches upon your original perception, and in this way you may come into many insights that will be of lasting value to you: but the end product you intended to develop, the realization in the material world of that which you perceived in the astral, may have lost the astral root that assures its place in the scheme of things.

Only too often an inventor has to hear the words, "If you had placed this before the public a year ago, or even months back, it would have had a great success: but now, ideas *have moved on. . . .* "

## Powerful action

How can you avoid this?

Certainly, speed and delicacy are called for in observing and acting upon any astral phenomenon. You should bear in mind, too, that *you, yourself,* by giving attention to this phenomenon will have tended to change it to some extent, depending upon your own preconceived ideas and attitude of mind. John Boslough, writing in *National Geographic* (May, 1985), tells us: "Observation not only affects reality, but in a way creates it. . . . "

The subject he is discussing is the scientific observation and measurement of *light,* a phenomenon that, while it is indeed of the material universe, partakes so much of the qualities of the astral world that we often refer to that world simply as "the astral light." In terms of physical science, it has long been debated whether light should be considered as composed of waves or of particles. We may suspect therefore that it is not strictly either, but what Boslough is here pointing out is that if you think of light as a particle, you can measure it as a particle and you can see it behaving as a particle: if you think of it as a "wave" you can measure it as a wave and you can see it behaving as a wave.

Jung, a number of years back, took the affectability of phenomena even further. He commented on the fact, which the experience of many workers in technical, medical, and other fields painfully verifies, that when research is conducted upon any new hypothesis that arouses enthusiasm, the resulting statistics—no matter how objectively gathered and tabulated—will, so long as the initial enthusiasm lasts, tend to run high in favor of the hypothesis. Then the percentage of bad results tends to rise again, the enthusiasm begins to wane, and the statistics begin their descent to average level.

When you know of these facts in relation to the material world, you begin to perceive the extreme delicacy of touch that is required in your contacts and investigations in the astral. *However, you can take powerful action to help yourself here. Just as the astral world can act upon the material, so the mental and spiritual worlds can act upon the astral.*

Here, then, is a simple technique for your use when in projection, designed to give strength and durability to the particular phenomenon that you choose to be the astral root of your project.

## *Charging a Phenomenon with Light*

1. When in the course of your astral explorations you discover something that particularly interests you, something you want to develop in the material world, or something you feel would be good in this world just as it is, position yourself so as to face it directly.

2. Next, by a mental act, bring into being a line of vibrant and luminous whiteness around the object. Here, when you are in a state of projected consciousness, you can instantly create this circle of astral light and see it directly in its bright and marvelous reality. It will be used to contain the power you are about to set in motion, and you should bring it into being with this purpose in mind.

3. Now be aware of your crown center, the sphere of light situated just above your head. In a general way, this will be like the image of your crown center as you were earlier directed to visualize it for the *Setting apart of the place* and the *Foundation technique*. Here, however, upon the astral plane, you have in relation to this sphere your astral perception of the Light of your Higher Self; that nucleus of Light

which, itself divine, is your special bond with the eternal Life of the entire universe.

4. Become more and more aware of this Light, aware of more and more of its glorious brilliance and radiance, as it streams forth a warm and all-pervading effulgence that surrounds you and fills every part of your being.

   Welcome it, breathe it in, feel it coursing through you until you are entirely saturated with its power, its bliss, its love.

5. Now direct your gaze to the object you have encircled with the vibrant white line. Look upon it with deep interest. You are making it part of your life, adopting it into your destiny.

6. Feel the wondrous light that fills you gradually passing from you to that object. The object becomes more luminous and radiant, until it darts forth bright rays to the bounds of the circle.

   You, yourself, correspondingly, become less and less aware of luminosity. Not that the presence of your Higher Self leaves you or is diminished to you, but because the purpose for which you brought this particular charging through to consciousness is being fulfilled in transferring the light to the contents of the circle.

   While this transferal is in progress, you should astrally say, or mentally affirm, something like:

   > *With the Light of my Higher Self I charge this object*
   > *(manifestation, happening, whatever) so that it remain*
   > *as an astral root for my work concerning it in the mate-*
   > *rial world.*

7. Continue for a short time to gaze at the light-filled contents of the circle; then return to your physical body, or give your attention to other wonders of the astral, as you will. The action you have performed will have locked the phenomenon in which you are interested by endowing it with more than astral reality and purpose.

   If you return to your body, there is no need for you to discontinue the formulation of the light above your head. If you are going to remain on the astral, see the sphere of light above the head of your astral light-envelope diminishing and disappearing.

# The person of power

The centers of light used in the *Foundation technique* belong to your astral body but they are not truly a part of your astral light-envelope, the vehicle of astral substance used by your projected consciousness in out-of-the-body experience. They can very effectively be awakened and utilized in relation to the astral light-envelope, however, just as the crown center is employed in the technique of *Charging a phenomenon with Light.*

The astral light-envelope is formed of the substance of your astral body, and is undifferentiated as to eyes, ears, or any other organs. You could use all of your faculties through any part of it, but through habit you can probably exercise each sense more effectively if you do so as in your physical body.

So, just as you will have accustomed yourself to using, while in your astral light-envelope, the faculties you associate with your physical body (you may, for instance, in the early stages of astral projection have had to go through the sensations of opening your eyes in order to see in your astral vehicle) now you can greatly extend the power and scope of your activities by practicing astrally the use of faculties associated with your astral body.

While on the astral, therefore, perform the *Foundation technique:* awakening the centers, bringing into being the central column of light, and mantling yourself in the golden radiance of your heart center. This will be a totally different experience from that of the visualized exercise performed while in your physical body; for your directed thoughts will become astral realities that are apparent to you, and you will be encompassed by living light and astral splendor.

To an extent your use of the *Foundation technique* while you are in a state of projection will engage the faculties of the astral level of your psyche, and communication between your astral body and your projected astral light-envelope will be amplified. This will certainly aid you in bringing over—through the silver cord—any special knowledge that may be required on a given occasion, especially if use of the technique is preceded by a mental formulation of your intention to receive that knowledge.

You probably have already realized how it can become second nature, with practice, to form your astral vehicle into a workable replica of a human person. You now have the means to make it a replica of a person of power, for you can use the energies of the centers in strong works of healing and other acts which would be hard either to plan or achieve through the dense veil of the material body.

# 16

# Assisted Projection

---

*Assisted projection—a viable work • The program*
*of preparation • A question of motivation*
*• Point of decision • Special circumstances*
*• Formula of assisted projection*
*• Involvement of astrosome and noemasome*

---

To draw another person out of the body to experience astral projection in full consciousness, be it a close friend, a lover, or simply a fellow student of the psychic mysteries, is a technique that is frequently spoken of but less often applied.

It is, however, a very workable proposition, provided that certain conditions are met.

For one thing, if you intend to assist a person in this manner, you must yourself be proficient in the art of astral projection. It is no good attempting to pull a person out of the body if you are unable to be astrally present to her or him, and fully in control of your astral faculties. For another thing, the person who is to be assisted must be properly prepared according to the standards of an accepted program for astral projection.

In the present instance, the basic program of preparation comprises the following:

- The *Setting apart of the place.*

- The *Foundation technique:* the procedure for awakening the energy centers of the astral body and enhancing the interaction of the psychic levels.

- The methods of drawing out, molding and re-absorbing astral substance, as in the techniques of the *First play, Forming the sphere of light, Sending an astral message* and *Sending a beneficent wish.*

- The procedures for creating, sending forth, recalling and reading a Watcher.

- The technique of reading the active Watcher.

- The methods of astral projection:
  (1) The stepping forth
  (2) Change of perspective
  (3) The going forth
  (4) The revolving formula

## Motivation

There is, furthermore, the question of motivation on both sides.

If there is sufficient motivation—it could be the desire on the part of a lover to be with you on the astral in order to attain a level of closeness impossible in earthly conditions; it could be the aspiration of a friend to share adventures and to explore astral realms of delight with you; it could be the fervent hope of a fellow student to be inducted by you into astral consciousness; and withal your own perception of the value of assisting that particular person to enter the astral light—then this again increases the chance of successfully pulling someone out of the body.

# A decision

A person who is to be assisted to go forth from the body must, from the outset of their study, have had a real dedication to the art of astral projection, and must have worked conscientiously through the preliminary disciplines, fully intending to achieve out-of-the-body experience by personal effort.

Someone, for instance, who has determined in the early stages of astral practice that too much effort is involved in the achievement of willed out-of-the-body experience, and who consequently determines to forego personal astral work in favor of being pulled out by a suitable practitioner of astral projection, is unlikely to prove a suitable candidate for the experiment.

As to the point at which the decision to assist a person to travel forth from the body is made, this will depend on various factors besides the preparedness of the candidate: the impelling need for teacher and student to perform joint astral work; the reciprocal energy of lovers that seeks astral expression and demands fulfillment *now*; an overwhelming sense of the *rightness* of assisting a friend to crown his or her study with vital and immediate experience. Although some people achieve early success with fully conscious astral projection, others can work conscientiously at the discipline for years with little apparent result. The dream life of such people may be immeasurably enriched through their endeavors, and their involuntary astral journeying may be frequent; but somehow they are not able to bring the technique of astral travel under the control of their rational mind and thereby achieve fully conscious, willed out-of-the-body experience. To assist a person who is in this situation to attain the freedom of willed astral experience could likewise prove to be a worthwhile and meaningful work.

# Special circumstances

It is recognized, of course, that circumstances can arise in which a person *may need* to be pulled out of the body without due preparation. In such an event the subject is certainly placed at a disadvantage, being left without knowledge of procedures for return to the physical body and for proper alignment of psychic levels, and being without actual experience of working with astral substance. It is, nonetheless, entirely feasible for an experienced practitioner to perform such a work with a novice, if there is sufficient cause. It may be for example that only direct astral experience could restore the subject to an overall and wholesome sense of perspective and to an appreciation of life's purpose. Or it may be that for some other deep reason, perhaps relating to factors of reincarnation, the astral practitioner is *called* to perform such a work. In general, however, to pull an unprepared person out of the body is not a procedure to be recommended.

## Formula of Assisted Projection
### The Traveler

1. A time of working being agreed on between the astral traveler and the one who is to be assisted to enter the astral world, the astral traveler performs the *Setting apart of the place* and then assumes the projection posture upon a bed, a mattress, or whatever.

### The Subject

2. The subject of the experiment, the person who is to be assisted to attain full astral consciousness, does not perform the *Setting apart of the place*. He or she reposes, however, in the projection posture and performs the *Foundation technique*.

3. Maintaining awareness of the golden aura that surrounds the physical body, the subject sees him- or herself as wearing an image of the physical body in silver-gray light, almost like a second skin.

4. Concentrating the attention upon this surrounding astral light-envelope, the subject becomes strongly aware of the silver-gray figure and of the outer aura of golden light.

5. The subject then transfers awareness into the astral simulacrum of the self thus formed, so that awareness of the physical body is less-

ened and consciousness of the silver-gray figure and the golden aura
is heightened.

### The Traveler

6. The astral traveler performs the *Foundation technique,* and then
   projects consciousness onto the astral plane by the preferred
   method. In the astral light-envelope, the astral practitioner then
   travels to the subject of the working.

### The Subject

7. The subject, meanwhile, maintaining awareness of the silver-gray
   figure and the golden aura, makes a mental affirmation, such as:

   > *I will achieve fully conscious astral projection, through*
   > *the help of . . .*

### The Traveler

8. The astral practitioner, having arrived at the physical location of the
   subject, performs astrally the *Setting apart of the place.*

9. The astral practitioner next approaches the physical body of the
   subject and reposes his or her astral light-envelope above it, face-to-
   face, in a horizontal position.

10. In this position, the astral practitioner speaks astrally to the subject,
    or mentally formulates, the following or similar words:

    > *Awaken to greater life, O beloved, and travel with me*
    > *upon the astral.*

11. The practitioner then formulates a clockwise-revolving sheath of
    light encompassing both of them horizontally. Within this light he
    or she takes the astral hands of the subject, or embraces him or her
    with one hand supporting the head and the other the waist (as may
    seem appropriate).

12. The practitioner repeats the call to the subject:

    > *Awaken to greater life, O beloved, and travel with me*
    > *upon the astral.*

13. The astral practitioner then moves away from the physical body of the subject, ascending swiftly in horizontal plane, and still holding the subject's astral hands or continuing the embrace.

14. At a distance of about eight feet from the physical body of the subject, the astral practitioner disengages the hands or discontinues the embrace.

15. The practitioner now repeats the call for the third time:

    *Awaken to greater life, O beloved, and travel with me*
    *upon the astral.*

16. After allowing a period of time for support and companionship, and during which means of communication between practitioner and subject can be explored and tested (mental communication, astral speech), the practitioner should by word or gesture bid the subject to return to his or her physical body. When the subject has done this and returned to earthly consciousness the practitioner should depart, likewise returning to the physical body or proceeding to other astral work.

### The Subject

17. The subject, having returned to the body, should conclude the operation with the *Foundation technique*, to ensure proper alignment of the levels of his or her psyche.

## An astral catalyst

From this time, the subject will have the power to project at will, and in full consciousness.

Although the technique given here consists in drawing forth the astral light-envelope, the prepared circumstances of the work and the concentration of consciousness on the part of the subject within the astral figure of the self will ensure that both the astrosome and the noemasome are engaged in the operation of assisted projection; as, indeed, will the catalyst provided by the real pulling out of the subject's astral substance.

For the last reason, it is preferable that this work should be conducted by you while you are out of the body in the astral world, rather than while you are in the body in the material world; for you will thus have the advantage of seeing more clearly what you are doing, of working directly with the reality of astral substance, and of controlling events in a manner which will ensure a true and successful outcome of the process.

# 17

# Animals and the Astral

---

*Kinship with animals • Instinctual and emotional life*
*• Reasoning ability in animals • Levels of intelligence*
*• Artificial elementals and animals*
*• Human guidance • The group aura*
*• Astral companions*

---

A book of this kind—on how to achieve out-of-the-body experience, on various aspects of that experience, of astral substance and the astral world—must necessarily be concerned mainly with human beings.

For one thing, it's intended to be read by humans. For another thing, the complexities about rational and subrational consciousness, about moral issues, about doubts, fables, and hearsay of one sort and another—all clouding the main themes to some extent—are entirely human problems and are of the most part of human creation.

However, the astral world has other dwellers and visitors besides humans. Of these, something is said in different parts of this book about the elementals. Something needs now to be said about the animals also.

# Humans and animals

Some humans have a great love for animals. A much greater number of humans turn to the company of animals (as some others turn to the company of elementals) for refreshment and relaxation away from the exacting requirements of human society, the real or implied censoriousness that they learn to fear from childhood onward. Indeed, the old defiant jingle that says, "Sticks and stones may break my bones, but words can never hurt me!" is proved seriously untrue when research has shown that any exchange of speech with a fellow human, even a child, will always to some extent step up one's blood pressure.

For these reasons and more, including the beauty and the swift, balanced movement of animals and the fascination of their ways of life, a great many people feel a conscious kinship with animals and are drawn to find out all they can about them; so that this rarely treated subject, the relationship of animals to the astral world, is a matter of considerable interest—and may also throw some valuable light upon our understanding of ourselves.

# Faithful friends

Particularly among folk who live in settled circumstances, one fairly often hears of a favorite cat or dog who, after death, has on various occasions been seen, heard, or simply felt unmistakably—in the literal, tactile sense—in the family home. Sometimes these occasions are as inconsequent as the comings and goings of any incarnate pet; sometimes there seems to be a definite pattern and purpose to them, indications quite often of some kind of impending change that the human members of the household don't yet foresee.

# Instinctual perceptions

None of this is, in itself, very surprising. Animals are much more at home on the astral plane than unpracticed humans are, because the instinctual and emotional levels of being occupy so much more of their life experience. The highly developed etheric sight of animals is well-known, and the etheric development of their senses of hearing and of smell are probably even more highly developed, in proportion to the importance of those senses to them on the material level. It is a matter that does not seem to strike human observers when they remark on animals' *uncanny* psychic perception.

## Animal intelligence

At the same time, those people are either badly mistaken or badly prejudiced who deny that animals have any reasoning ability. Except in a panic situation, an animal considering a leap, for instance, can sometimes be seen visibly considering the distance and the best prospect of success, and glancing down, too, to see if the possibility of failure holds any danger. Again, anyone who has seen a bull or a stallion figuring out the mechanism of a latch, or the convolutions of a knot, will be hard put to explain how instinct could even attempt to cope with such man-made problems.

The animal is often defeated by having only teeth, or the points of a horn, with which to put the matter to practical trial; but that's another story, and a mighty long one.

## Intelligence and individual identity

One mustn't, of course, go to the other extreme and credit animals with levels of thought that would require a brain of human standard to support them. Yet there is some intelligence in a good many living creatures, varying with species and with individual ability, and generally of a higher level than a lot of humans would like to acknowledge.

This question of intelligence is mentioned here because it has a distinct relationship to what happens on the astral plane. Sometimes (to digress by way of illustration) a human will create what may be termed an *artificial elemental* and charge it with some particular purpose to fulfill. It can be in the form of one of the astral globes already discussed, or it could be in the shape of an animal or a human figure. It may be created to carry a message simply; or to gather news; or to guard a person (such as a child) in a specific situation; or to diffuse a happy mood at a party, or some such thing.

This artificial entity—it is, of course, composed of the sender's astral substance—can very well carry out a simple instruction. *But it can't think, can't use any initiative.* Because it is purely astral and because its creator's conscious intelligent mind doesn't go with it, it can do no more than it was initially programmed to do.

When the job is done, therefore, the creator of the thing has to recall it, deprogram it and re-absorb it. If this proper procedure were not followed, the form would just drift about on the astral, progressively disintegrating for sure, but meanwhile liable to absorb and give expression to any stray astral impulse that may be around.

But this doesn't happen with the animal visitants we've been discussing. They remain their own selves, with their individual characters and distinctive ways. They are not just packaged instincts. Their intelligence may not be great by human standards, but it is enough to allow the individual animal psyche to maintain itself in the astral world without losing its identity or sense of continuity.

## When animal-lovers talk

Certain types of stories are always being told about domestic animals, of no matter what species: on the one hand, of their unexpected tokens of intelligence; on the other hand, of their high degree of psychic rapport with their human associates, and with nonhumans, frequently of different species from themselves. There are also stories of their survival after death, showing as clear evidence as can be given for any human being.

Here and there some narrator may exaggerate a little, whether consciously or otherwise, out of affection and pride, but mostly what is said accords with common knowledge and makes credible sense in the light of our understanding of the astral and of psychic powers. Particularly in the area of psychic communication, a great deal concerning animals is demonstrated and proved.

# Effects of human guidance

The question arises: does human company and guidance help develop the nature of an animal?—in the matter of intelligence, for example?

Undoubtedly this is the case. Constant affection and communication from a trusted human person will certainly develop the faculties and bring out the intelligence of most animals. Whether intelligence can ever be truly increased beyond its initial level, even in humans, is a moot point; but certainly, for humans and other species alike, the establishment of acceptable codes of communication, the fact that communication is desired, and observation of the leader's behavior, will help bring out the existing level of intelligence to its optimum.

The same is true of psychic communication. Indeed, the development of intelligence most probably rests upon a basis of psychic faculties, recognized or unrecognized. In many instances, an animal is aware of what you intend to do, before watching carefully to see how you do it.

Among humans these facts can frequently be observed: both the interrelationship (in certain individuals) of intelligence and psychic ability, and the stimulating effect (in people of all sorts) of the company of individuals of higher development, whether of rational or nonrational faculties.

The interrelationship of intelligence and the nonrational faculties is a very dicey proposition. A number of leaders in the world of commerce owe their success to a blend of acute intelligence and very distinct psychic perceptions. On the other hand, one comes across individuals of uncanny psychic powers who couldn't follow through the simplest piece of logical reasoning. It is the people in the great middle range of the scale who have the toughest task: those whose attention, if they don't take care, will be entirely absorbed in keeping abreast of the rational requirements of everyday living.

Regarding the other question, about the stimulating effect of the company of individuals of higher development, whether rational or nonrational, the evidence is, fortunately, unanimous.

Retarded people can benefit immensely through not being limited to the company of the retarded, and a truly concerned teacher or leader can often discover, in a slow or discouraged child or adult, unexpected talents that will, in turn, open up the way for yet further developments. The awakening of interest, of a desire for knowledge or ability, is the great key to be sought.

Similarly, intelligent people can be perceptibly stimulated to higher attainment through the company of the more intelligent. This has been seen many times. The whole concept of the literary or artistic salon, for instance, is based on the idea that the celebrities meeting there will enjoy, not merely meeting each other, but also the exhilarating and wit-sharpening effect of the conversation.

## The group aura

Undoubtedly, for humans and nonhumans alike, the group aura is a most important factor in producing these various effects. Among humans, one class of children can develop a markedly different overall character from another class in the same school. The same can be observed among human communities of all kinds: offices, apartment buildings, sports teams. A ball player transferred from another team may take some time to integrate with the group aura of his new team; if he's transferred too many times he may cease to integrate at all.

For wild or semi-wild animals the unit or the group may be the family, the herd, or the pack, according to species. For a domestic animal, the unit is usually the human family; although this may have a variable value when other animals are also part of the group, as one sees when dog and cat gang up to raid the larder shelf or the kitchen counter.

Strange instances are recorded, too, when an animal not only becomes accepted as a member in a group of different species, but also adopts the living and feeding habits of that species. Occasionally a sheep dog, instead of guarding and herding the sheep, will consider itself as one of them and will flee in their midst at the threat of danger. A horse is also recorded as having identified with a flock of sheep, and living as a sheep thenceforward.

One possible explanation of these things is that the errant animal was, in a previous incarnation, a member of the species that is now adopted. That seems to be the most reasonable explanation in instances where the species that is adopted is not physically present. But, where there is a flock of sheep, a herd of deer, a warren of rabbits, or whatever the adopted species may be, the compulsive power of the group aura to instill certain ways of life and behavior must be considered a main factor.

## Human influence and astral individualization

Thinking of these matters from a theoretical viewpoint, we could suppose human nurturing must give the domestic animal a considerable advantage in consciousness of self on the astral plane, whether in formulation of ideas, in projection of consciousness, or after death.

There is, certainly, an amount of evidence that seems to go that way, and there is, as well, tradition and the experience of the occultist.

## Astral company

To travel upon the astral plane in the company of a favorite pet can be a richly rewarding experience. There is the delight, for instance, not only of the loving friendship in itself, but also of exploration of the animal's astral domain, of its favorite otherworldly interests and sometimes, too, of its other astral, or out-of-the-body, companions.

You may perhaps have a special friend, a beloved cat, say, or a dog, who is able to project and who, already, regularly awaits you in the astral world—just like the witch's familiar!

## Calling to the friend

It may be that you may have a loving and faithful pet who, to your knowledge, does not project and whose astral development in this regard you would like to encourage.

In that case you can certainly visit your animal companion astrally, preferably while it sleeps; and you can call to it to come forth. You can do this on numerous occasions until you achieve success. What you cannot do, however, is to assist the animal to achieve astral projection by pulling it out of the body, for that is a procedure that involves the cooperation of reasoning faculties and the will. Nonetheless, because of the innate psychic ability of most animals, the chances are that your pet will very soon get the message and will join you upon the astral.

It will not always be possible to share your adventures, however, for whereas you can learn to ascend to higher planes or to travel into the past, your pet cannot, and your times together on the astral will be spent in the present, and in the domain of the natural world.

# 18

# The Protecting Light

---

*The Light of your Higher Self—Source of protection*
*• Awakening the Light*
*• Surrounding yourself with power, bliss, and love*
*• Human or nonhuman influence • Psychic wholeness*

---

While upon the astral you may sometimes find it necessary to protect yourself from the influence or the attention of inimical beings or forces, human or nonhuman.

The greatest source of protection that you have in this regard, and that you may call upon at any time, is the Light of your Higher Self. Your Higher Self, in the essence of its being, resides in the spiritual world, but its influence reaches through all the worlds to hold you in loving and secure embrace.

Two methods are provided in this book whereby you may invoke the presence, the protection, and the power of the Light of your Higher Self.

The first, and major, method is *Awakening the Light*, as given in the *Setting apart of the place*. The points of the technique, for astral use, are:

- Turn your attention to the source of Light and Life. Contemplate it and aspire to it.

- Conceive of yourself as increasing in stature, as becoming vast.

- Maintaining the formulation of immensity, visualize a globe of brilliant white light just above your head.

- See the luminosity of the globe increasing, permeating your entire being and surrounding you with an aura of light.

This technique should be employed in its fullness, as earlier presented in chapter 3.

The second method is given in the technique of *Charging a phenomenon with Light*:

- Be aware of your crown center, the sphere of light situated just above your head. Here, upon the astral plane, you have in relation to this sphere your astral perception of the Light of your Higher Self; that nucleus of Light which, itself divine, is your special bond with the eternal Life of the entire universe.

- Become more and more aware of this Light, aware of more and more of its glorious brilliance and radiance, as it streams forth a warm and all-pervading effulgence that surrounds you and fills every part of your being.

- Welcome it, breathe it in, feel it coursing through you until you are entirely saturated with its power, its bliss, its love.

## Choosing the method

Where it is apparent to you that you are confronted with an inimical nonhuman being or force, you should employ the procedure of *Awakening the Light*. This method of invoking the Light of your Higher Self, involving as it does your aspiration toward, and response to, the spiritual world, is appropriate to works of protection from nonhuman influences.

Where an inimical force is discerned to be of human origin, the second method of invoking the Light of your Higher Self should be used. Here, the emphasis is not so much upon aspiration to the spiritual world as upon reception of the outpoured gifts of light that come to you from the inmost level of your psyche; and so, in context, this method is applicable to what may be termed "the area of human concerns."

## Wonderful potential

One of the greatest rewards to be expected from out-of-the-body experience is the sense of psychic wholeness that will increasingly pervade your life as your contact with and understanding of the deeper levels of your psyche intensifies.

The technique of *Awakening the Light* offers a particularly valuable resource in this regard, and it should be undertaken by you on a regular basis, and as a work in its own right in the astral world; for by means of it you can enter into an increasing awareness of the presence and reality of your inmost self.

In this, your life will be immeasurably enriched, your heart will become ever more responsive to the inspirations and promptings of the spiritual world, and you will in time come to travel, truly and always, within the ambience of the Protecting Light.

# Bibliography

Baker, Dr. Douglas M. *Practical Techniques of Astral Projection.* Wellingborough: The Aquarian Press, 1977.

Brennan, J. H. *The Astral Projection Workbook.* Wellingborough: The Aquarian Press, 1989; New York: Sterling Publishing Co., Inc., 1990.

———. *Time Travel: A New Perspective.* St. Paul, Minn.: Llewellyn Worldwide, 1997.

Crookall, Robert. *The Mechanisms of Astral Projection.* Moradabad: Darshana International, 1969.

Denning, Melita, and Osborne Phillips. *The Llewellyn Practical Guide to Astral Projection.* St. Paul, Minn.: Llewellyn Worldwide, 1979.

Frost, Gavin and Yvonne. *Astral Travel.* London: Granada Publishing Ltd., 1982.

Green, Celia. *Out-of-the-Body Experiences.* Oxford: Institute for Psychophysical Research, 1968.

Leadbeater, Charles. *The Astral Plane.* Wheaton: Theosophical Publishing House, 1933.

McCoy, Edain. *Astral Projection for Beginners.* St. Paul, Minn.: Llewellyn Worldwide, 1999.

Monroe, Robert A. *Far Journeys.* Garden City, N.Y.; Doubleday, 1985.

———. *Journeys Out of the Body.* New York: Doubleday and Co., Inc., 1971.

Muldoon, Sylvan and Hereward Carrington. *The Phenomena of Astral Projection*. London: Rider and Co., 1951.

Rogo, Scott. *Leaving the Body: A Complete Guide to Astral Projection*. Englewood Cliffs, N.J.: Prentice-Hall, 1983.

Slate, Joe H., Ph.D. *Astral Projection and Psychic Epowerment: Techniques for Mastering the Out-of-Body Experience*. St. Paul, Minn.: Llewellyn Worldwide, 1998.

Webster, Richard. *Astral Travel for Beginners*. St. Paul, Minn.: Llewellyn Worldwide, 1998.

# Index

92–93, 100, 109, 113, 120,
123–124, 131, 138, 144, 151
Pure radiance formula, 111,
118, 121–122

reabsorption, 44, 47, 52–53, 55,
62–63
recalling, 49, 52–53, 55, 79,
134
reincarnation, 136
Return, the, 9, 33, 44, 52–53,
61–63, 69, 72, 74, 81, 93,
115, 123, 130, 136, 138
revolving formula, 59, 134

Setting apart of the place, 15,
19, 22–23, 28, 40, 42, 45, 47,
51, 53, 56–59, 86, 92, 129,
134, 136–137, 149
silver cord, the, 52–53, 131
simulacrum, 49, 56–57, 59, 136

soul-stuff, 1–3
Soul-world, 7
Sphere of light, 21, 39, 42,
46–47, 122–123, 129–130,
134, 150
spiritual energy, 19, 23
Spiritual Sun, 119–120,
122–123
spiritual teacher, 68
Spiritual world, 9–12, 149–151
Spiritualist, 32
stepping forth, 56, 134

twin psychism, 99, 108

vibration, 66

Watcher, 49–54, 56, 58, 134
Westenra, Lucy, 29, 34
White Light, 20–22, 27, 150
wholeness, 1, 26, 117, 127, 149,
151

# ORDER LLEWELLYN BOOKS TODAY!

*Llewellyn publishes hundreds of books on your favorite subjects! To get these exciting books, including the ones on the following pages, check your local bookstore or order them directly from Llewellyn.*

## Order Online:
Visit our website at www.llewellyn.com, select your books, and order them on our secure server.

## Order by Phone:
- Call toll-free within the U.S. at 1-877-NEW-WRLD (1-877-639-9753) Call toll-free within Canada at 1-866-NEW-WRLD (1-866-639-9753)
- We accept VISA, MasterCard, and American Express

## Order by Mail:
Send the full price of your order (MN residents add 7% sales tax) in U.S. funds, plus postage & handling to:

**Llewellyn Worldwide**
**P.O. Box 64383, Dept. 0-7387-0279-X**
**St. Paul, MN 55164-0383, U.S.A.**

## Postage & Handling:
**Standard** (U.S., Mexico, & Canada). If your order is:
Up to $25.00, add $3.50
$25.01 - $48.99, add $4.00
$49.00 and over, FREE STANDARD SHIPPING
(Continental U.S. orders ship UPS. AK, HI, PR, & P.O. Boxes ship USPS 1st class. Mex. & Can. ship PMB.)

**International Orders:**
**Surface Mail:** For orders of $20.00 or less, add $5 plus $1 per item ordered. For orders of $20.01 and over, add $6 plus $1 per item ordered.

**Air Mail:**
*Books:* Postage & Handling is equal to the total retail price of all books in the order.
*Non-book items:* Add $5 for each item.

*Orders are processed within 2 business days. Please allow for normal shipping time.*
*Postage and handling rates subject to change.*

## The Astral Projection Kit
### *Denning & Phillips*

When you can perform astral projection, you temporarily break the bonds holding mind and body together so that you can travel through space and time . . . obtain higher knowledge . . . communicate with those on the astral planes . . . and more! Here is a complete kit to aid you in successful and conscious astral travel! You receive a 90-minute cassette tape, the book *The Llewellyn Practical Guide to Astral Projection*, and a meditation card with instructions to serve as your doorway into the astral planes. Easy step-by-step exercises allow you to safely travel the astral plane to renew your physical and emotional health, mental powers, spiritual attainment, and activate the development of psychic faculties.

**0-87542-199-7, 252-pp. book 5¼ x 8, Boxed set**      **$24.95**
**90-minute audio tape; meditation card with instructions**

# Practical Guide
# to Psychic Powers:
## Awaken Your Sixth Sense
### *Denning & Phillips*

Because you are missing out on so much without them! Who has not dreamed of possessing powers to move objects without physically touching them, to see at a distance or into the future, to know another's thoughts, to read the past of an object or person, or to find water or mineral wealth by dowsing?

This book is a complete course—teaching you step-by-step how to develop the powers that actually have been yours since birth. Psychic powers are a natural part of your mind; by expanding your mind in this way, you will gain health and vitality, emotional strength, greater success in your daily pursuits, and a new understanding of your inner self.

You'll learn to play with these new skills, working with groups of friends to accomplish things you never would have believed possible. The text shows you how to make the equipment, do the exercises—many of them at any time, anywhere—and how to use your abilities to change your life and the lives of those close to you.

**0-87542-191-1, 216 pp., 5³⁄₁₆ x 8, illus.** **$9.95**

## Practical Guide to Creative Visualization

### For the Fulfillment of Your Desires

*Denning & Phillips*

All things you want must have their start in your mind. The average person uses very little of the full creative power that is potentially his or hers. It's like the power locked in the atom—it's all there, but you have to learn to release it and apply it constructively.

If you can see it . . . in your mind's eye . . . you will have it! It's true: you can have whatever you want, but there are "laws" to mental creation that must be followed. The power of the mind is not limited to, nor limited by, the material world. *Creative Visualization* enables humans to reach beyond, into the invisible world of astral and spiritual forces.

Some people apply this innate power without actually knowing what they are doing, and achieve great success and happiness; most people, however, use this same power, again unknowingly, incorrectly, and experience bad luck, failure, or, at best, an unfulfilled life.

This book changes that. Through an easy series of step-by-step, progressive exercises, your mind is applied to bring desire into realization! Wealth, power, success, happiness, even psychic powers . . . even what we call magickal power and spiritual attainment . . . all can be yours. You can easily develop this completely natural power, and correctly apply it, for your immediate and practical benefit.

**0-87542-183-0, 264 pp. 5³⁄₁₆ x 8**     **$9.95**
**Spanish edition, 1-56718-204-6**

# Practical Guide to Psychic Self-Defense and Well-being

*Denning & Phillips*

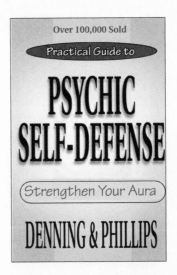

Psychic well-being and psychic self-defense are two sides of the same coin, just as are physical health and resistance to disease. Each person (and every living thing) is surrounded by an electromagnetic force field, or aura, that can provide the means to psychic self-defense and to dynamic well-being. This book explores the world of very real "psychic warfare" of which we are all victims.

Every person in our modern world is subjected to psychic stress and psychological bombardment: advertising promotions that play upon primitive emotions, political and religious appeals that work on feelings of insecurity and guilt, noise, threats of violence and war, news of crime and disaster, etc.

This book shows the nature of genuine psychic attacks—ranging from actual acts of black magic to bitter jealousy and hate—and the reality of psychic stress, the structure of the psyche and its interrelationship with the physical body. It shows how each person must develop his weakened aura into a powerful defense-shield, thereby gaining both physical protection and energetic well-being that can extend to protection from physical violence, accidents . . . even ill health.

**0-87542-190-3, 264 pp., 5³⁄₁₆ x 8, illus.**          **$9.95**

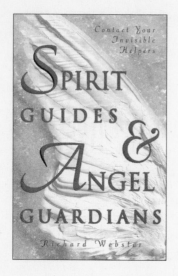

## Spirit Guides & Angel Guardians
### Contact Your Invisible Helpers
*Richard Webster*

They come to our aid when we least expect it, and they disappear as soon as their work is done. Invisible helpers are available to all of us; in fact, we all regularly receive messages from our guardian angels and spirit guides but usually fail to recognize them. This book will help you to realize when this occurs. And when you carry out the exercises provided, you will be able to communicate freely with both your guardian angels and spirit guides.

You will see your spiritual and personal growth take a huge leap forward as soon as you welcome your angels and guides into your life. This book contains numerous case studies that show how angels have touched the lives of others, just like yourself. Experience more fun, happiness, and fulfillment than ever before. Other people will also notice the difference as you become calmer, more relaxed, and more loving than ever before.

Learn the important differences between a guardian angel and a spirit guide; invoke the Archangels for help in achieving your goals; discover the different ways your guardian angel speaks to you; and create your own guardian angel from within. You can use your guardian angel to aid in healing yourself and others and find your life's purpose through your guardian angel. Use your spirit guides to help you release negative emotions, call on specific guides for nurturing, support, fun, motivation, wisdom, and visit your guides through past-life regression

1-56718-795-1, 368 pp., 5¾₆ x 8                    $9.95
Spanish edition, 1-56718-789-2

# How to Meet & Work with Spirit Guides

*Ted Andrews*

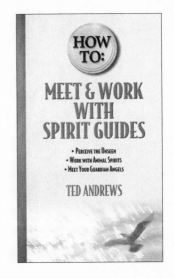

We often experience spirit contact in our lives but fail to recognize it for what it is. Now you can learn to access and attune to beings such as guardian angels, nature spirits and elementals, spirit totems, archangels, gods and goddesses—as well as family and friends after their physical death.

Contact with higher soul energies strengthens the will and enlightens the mind. Through a series of simple exercises, you can safely and gradually increase your awareness of spirits and your ability to identify them. You will learn to develop an intentional and directed contact with any number of spirit beings. Discover meditations to open up your subconscious. Learn which acupressure points effectively stimulate your intuitive faculties. Find out how to form a group for spirit work, use crystal balls, perform automatic writing, attune your aura for spirit contact, use sigils to contact the great archangels, and much more! Read *How to Meet and Work with Spirit Guides* and take your first steps through the corridors of life beyond the physical.

**0-87542-008-7, 192 pp., mass market, illus.** **$5.99**

## Astral Travel for Beginners
### Transcend Time and Space with Out-of-Body Experiences
*Richard Webster*

Astral projection, or the out-of-body travel, is a completely natural experience. You have already astral traveled thousands of times in your sleep, you just don't remember it when you wake up. Now, you can learn how to leave your body at will, be fully conscious of the experience, and remember it when you return.

The exercises in this book are carefully graded to take you step-by-step through an actual out-of-body experience. Once you have accomplished this, it becomes easier and easier to leave your body. That's why the emphasis in this book is on your first astral travel.

The ability to astral travel can change your life. You will have the freedom to go anywhere and do anything. You can explore new worlds, go back and forth through time, make new friends, and even find a lover on the astral planes. Most importantly, you will find that you no longer fear death as you discover that you are indeed a spiritual being independent of your physical body.

By the time you have finished the exercises in this book you will be able to leave your body and explore the astral realms with confidence and total safety.

**1-56718-796-X, 256 pp., 5³⁄₁₆ x 8**                        **$9.95**

# How to Communicate with Spirits

### *Elizabeth Owens*

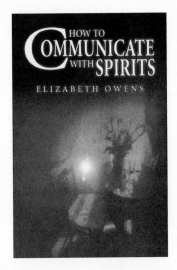

*Spiritualist mediums share their fascinating experiences with the "other side."*

Nowhere else will you find such a wealth of anecdotes from noted professional mediums residing within a Spiritualist community. Real-life psychics shed light on spirit entities, spirit guides, relatives who are in spirit, and communication with all of those on the spirit side of life.

You will explore the different categories of spirit guidance, and you will hear from the mediums themselves about their first contacts with the spirit world, as well as the various phenomena they have encountered. In this book, noted mediums residing within a Spiritualist community share their innermost experiences, opinions, and advice regarding spirit communication. It includes instructions for table tipping, automatic writing, and meditating to make contact with spirits. This is a book for anyone interested in developing and understanding spiritual gifts.

**1-56718-530-4, 240 pp., 5³⁄₁₆ x 8**                    **$9.95**

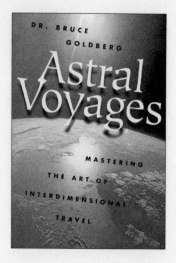

## Astral Voyages
### Mastering the Art of Interdimensional Travel
#### *Dr. Bruce Goldberg*

Free yourself from the limitations of the earth plane and the laws of space and time. *Astral Voyages* presents more than 65 exercises that train you to safely leave your physical body and return un-harmed from explorations of the upper astral plane and the causal, mental, or etheric realms. You might even venture to the soul plane and observe the process of selecting your next lifetime!

Dr. Goldberg unveils his paradigm of the 13 dimensions, developed from 25 years of experience with hypnotic regression, progression and out-of-body experiences. Specific scripts train you for guided imagery astral voyage, lucid dreaming, accessing the Akashic records, cabalistic projection, and advanced techniques such as the Witch's Cradle and the 37-Degree Technique used by the ancient Egyptians. Other topics include astral entities, astral sex, astral healing, and scientific studies on astral voyaging.

**1-56718-308-5, 240 pp., 6 x 9**                                    **$12.95**

## Astral Projection
## for Beginners
### *Edain McCoy*

Enter a world in which time and space
have no meaning or influence. This is the
world of the astral plane, an ethereal, unseen realm often perceived as parallel to
and interpenetrating our physical world.
*Astral Projection for Beginners* shows you
how to send your consciousness at will to these other places, then bring
it back with full knowledge of what you have experienced.

Explore the misconceptions and half-truths that often impede the
beginner, and create a mental atmosphere in which you become free to
explore the universe both inside and outside your consciousness. This
book offers six different methods for you to try: general transfer of
consciousness, projecting through the chakras, meditating towards astral separation, guided meditation, using symbolic gateways, and stepping out of your dreams. Ultimately you will be able to condition your
mind to allow you to project at will.

**1-56718-625-4, 256 pp., 5³⁄₁₆ x 8**                    **$9.95**